Early Praise for
Divine Nobodies

"I am tempted to say that Jim Palmer could well be the next Donald Miller, but what they have in common, along with an honest spirituality and extraordinary skill as storytellers, is a unique voice. So I might instead say that one of our best young writers in the future may well be called the next Jim Palmer. *Divine Nobodies* is a delight to read, and it did good for my soul to read it."

> — **Brian McLaren,**
> Author of
> *The Secret Message of Jesus*

"Jim Palmer has written a winsome, thought-provoking, and highly readable narrative—it's about being Christian and about being who God has created you to be. Jim obviously knows who he is, and he's a keen observer of humanity, which is why this book hits home. I'm happy to self-identify as a 'divine nobody.'"

> — **Tony Jones,**
> National Coordinator of
> Emergent Village
> (www.emergentvillage.com)
> and Author of *The Sacred Way*

"As soon as I saw the title of this book, I had a strong feeling I was going to like it. I had no idea that I would be giving away loose-leaf chapters to friends before I had even finished reading it. Jim Palmer might be at the head of the pack of the new 'Evanradicals.'"

> — **Oteil Burbridge,**
> Bass player, The Allman
> Brothers Band

"You hold in your hands an amazing story of a broken man finding freedom in all the right places—in God's work in the lives of some extraordinarily ordinary people around him. You will thrill to this delightful blend of gut-wrenching honesty and laugh-out-loud hilarity, and in the end you'll find God much closer, the body of Christ far bigger, and your own journey far clearer than you ever dreamed."

— Wayne Jacobsen,
Author of
Authentic Relationships

"I love this book! Coming from a non-church, non-functional, non-connected family I see myself as being a divine nobody in the hands of God. When we come to see ourselves as 'divine nobodies' we see the divine in 'all-bodies.'"

—John O'Keefe,
Founder of
www.ginkworld.net

Divine Nobodies

Divine Nobodies

Shedding Religion to Find God
(and the unlikely people who help you)

jim palmer

W Publishing Group
A Division of Thomas Nelson Publishers
Since 1798

www.wpublishinggroup.com

Published by W Publishing Group, a division of Thomas Nelson, Inc., P.O. Box 141000, Nashville, Tennessee 37214.

Scripture quotations are from the following sources:

The Holy Bible, New International Version (NIV). Copyright ©1973, 1978, 1984, International Bible Society. Used by permission of Zondervan.

The Message (MSG), copyright © 1993, 1994, 1995, 1996, 2000, 2001, 2002. Used by permission of NavPress Publishing Group.

The Amplified Bible (AMP), Expanded Edition, copyright © 1987 by The Zondervan Corporation and The Lockman Foundation. All rights reserved.

Library of Congress Cataloging-in-Publication Data

Palmer, Jim, 1964–
    Divine nobodies : shedding religion to find God (and the unlikely people who help you) / Jim Palmer.
        p. cm.
    ISBN-10: 0-8499-1398-5
    ISBN-13: 978-0-8499-1398-3
    1. Palmer, Jim, 1964– . 2. Christian biography. I. Title.
BR1725.P225A3 2006
277.3'0830922—dc22
[B]   2006012455

Printed in the United States of America

06 07 08 09 10 RRD 6 5 4 3 2 1

Contents

Pseudo-Introduction

(or The Thing That Sort of Seems Like an Introduction but Is a Pretty Poor Excuse for One)

YOU WILL EVENTUALLY SEE THIS BOOK HAS TWO INTRODUCTIONS, the Pseudo-Introduction and the Real Introduction. Having not yet said anything, I have already broken one of the publishing world's ten commandments: "Thou shalt not have two introductions." Both introductions are essential, which begs the question, Why didn't I just make them chapters and not have to write this paragraph? After all, some people, probably most people, skip the introduction in search of the good stuff. Instead, what I ended up with is two introductions for them to skip and a grim warning under the chapter 1 title begging the reader not to skip them. Two intros cost me two fingers, one for each commandment broken, the second being, "Thou shalt not tell the reader how to read his or her book."

I wanted to write a novel. I have long believed fiction is the highest evolved form of communication. My Virginia Tech hat is off to anyone who has both the imagination and the skill for creative writing. For years, I consumed nonfiction books that stated plainly in systematic fashion how to do Christianity better. I got the mechanics of Christian living pretty well down. Then I got a wild hair and read Wendell Berry's novel *Jayber Crow*, which deeply affected me. I discovered that good fiction has a way of opening you up and is cathartic for the soul. Jesus's creative way of conveying truth through stories and parables has been a magnet drawing me more deeply into life with God in recent years. I would read anything written by Jesus, not to shortchange Wendell Berry, who is also near the top of my list.

Prolific fiction writers blow my mind. I have pieces of a novel in progress stored in multiple files all over my computer. One day I realized my "novel" was really a personal memoir. I didn't want to insult people who truly have enough original thinking to write fiction, so I decided to lay it down for now. I realize most novels are to some degree autobiographical. Mine was entirely, save names of people, places, and a few cosmetic changes, designed to cast doubt in the minds of the actual people I was writing about (e.g., brunette, fair-skinned "Pam" in real life became blonde, tanned "Patty" in the novel—yes, my skills of throwing people off the trail are truly astounding). I also realize there is the "creative nonfiction" tactic of inventing people and plots to say something with an artsy twist. Finally, it dawned on me that there was a real story needing to be told, and given my track record as a novelist, I should just stick to stating it plainly the best I could.

I was taught when reading books to "consider the source," which may not bode too well in my favor. So, I feel some sense of obligation to share certain things about myself that could dissuade you from reading any further. Here's a random list of facts about "me" (some of which I am embarrassed about but willing to own up to):

1. Windows 98 is the operating system on my primary computer, and I still use dial-up service to surf the Internet.

2. Our primary household television is a fifteen-inch TV/VCR combo complete with foil-wrapped rabbit ears because we don't have cable. We do have another TV in worse condition that I inherited from my grandma Palmer in Chatham, New Jersey. It has the distinction of getting FOX if you are willing to hold the antenna cord in just the right position, which is what I do each year to watch the World Series.

3. My favorite place in our home is our tiny one-car garage (SUVs need not apply), where I often sit in a rocking recliner contemplating mysteries of the universe and sometimes startling people walking by (our driveway is extremely short) who don't expect to see a guy "reclining" in his garage. Often there is an awkward moment while the person or persons decide whether to "wave" and speed up or do the "Hey there" or "How are you?" thing, which opens the possibility of having a conversation with some guy sitting in a recliner out in the garage. Good times.

4. I once angered a seminary professor to the point he promised to personally see to it I never occupied a ministry position within his denomination. Reaming me out behind closed doors, my suspicion was born that a fair number of people in professional ministry are psychotic and unstable. I never did occupy any position in his denomination.

5. During the Michael Jordan / Chicago Bulls championship dynasty, I often lost sleep (at times, lots of it) when the Bulls lost an important game. It gets worse. I cried when Michael Jordan retired the first time. I did a victory dance when he returned. I was distraught when he didn't dominate major-league baseball, and I wished there could have been one last Cinderella story playing for the Wizards. The truth is, something died in me the day I realized Michael Jordan was not the perfect hero and role model the little kid inside so

deeply needed him to be. I don't know why it was so important to me; nobody's perfect, not even MJ.

6. There are always two realities associated with virtually every home repair I attempt—they take twice as long and cost twice as much compared to asking my neighbor Mary Anne to do it, which is typically what I do now. God knows I need to live near someone who enjoys rebuilding weed eaters for relaxation.

7. I'm obsessive-compulsive. I have necessary routines, and certain things need to be done certain ways or I am out of sorts. It's harder for me to cope if there are dirty dishes in the sink. My condition isn't always a bad thing. I'm probably a more disciplined person than the average Joe, but sometimes I have to ask myself if getting up at the same time every day to be with God is because I love him or because my compulsivity demands it. Also, if you stare at me long enough, you will notice an assortment of tics and twitches. If you listen closely, you are likely to hear humming and other subtle vocal noises, all resulting from my condition of Tourette syndrome.

8. I am frightened by heights and things that spin or go fast. You couldn't pay me enough to ride a roller coaster, Ferris wheel, or those spinning cup things. I could never snow ski, because I would pass out riding the lift. I didn't think I was claustrophobic until the day I had a CAT scan and feared for my life. The nurse kept asking through the little microphone, "Are you okay?" I would reply, "I don't think so." She would say, "Just relax." And this went on until I finally decided to close my eyes and force my mind to figure out why my Braves consistently come unglued in the postseason (not to minimize their unrivaled winning ways otherwise).

9. I'm a sucker for feel-good, tearjerker movies. One day I noticed many of the movies I like involve a broken father-son

relationship, which somehow all works out in the end, like *Field of Dreams* and *October Sky*. I also like the zero-to-hero flicks like *Patch Adams, Mr. Holland's Opus, Forrest Gump, The Lord of the Rings*, and, yes, *Rocky* (that is, the first one . . . well, maybe the second one . . . okay, I also saw the third one . . . was there a fourth?). I also like off-the-beaten-path films that most people will never know exist. See *The Wild Parrots of Telegraph Hill* (it's worth Googling).

10. Something broke inside me the night I personally witnessed child prostitution for the first and last time. More later . . .

11. My daughter, Jessica, is six years old and showing signs of growing up. I'm not sure I really want her to continue. Sometimes she listens to her *Wee Sing* CD, and other times she asks to hear my U2, Switchfoot, or John Mayer stuff. (I've hidden my Kanye West CDs from her!) Things happen when you have kids. I find myself wanting to watch Clifford even when she's not around. My most fervent and desperate prayer lately is that she score her first goal in a soccer game. I often lie in bed at night thinking about all the reasons I love her and how much I don't want her to be hurt in this world. When she conks out in the backseat, I sometimes arrange the rearview mirror so I can see her. She looks like an angel when she's sleeping.

12. Then there's my wife, Pam, whom by this time I'm sure you pity by virtue of the previous eleven paragraphs. A very strong woman, I sometimes wonder if I could go on without her. She's my best friend, and all the crap of the world and my life seem silenced lying next to her in bed.

13. We have a high-maintenance cat named Daisy that is as old as dirt. For the past seven years, that cat has kept me from a good night's sleep. She always wants something in the middle

of the night and has me in mind to do her bidding. I act like she's a big nuisance, but when no one's around to see, I let her jump up in my lap and I love on her. Daisy and I have a mutual understanding about our relationship. We really like each other but have reasons for hiding our true feelings.

14. I feel things deeply. It's a part of me I try to hide, and I usually do a pretty good job of it. My emotions spill out at the oddest times. The 2005 Super Bowl commercial with weary soldiers returning home in an airport and people spontaneously thanking and applauding them choked me up so badly I had to leave the room . . . quickly. I was recently at a park with my daughter and noticed a mother going off on her little boy, berating him with terrible names. Even as I write this, I am fighting back emotion. I can't watch *The Tigger Movie* anymore because it wrecks me. (I won't even get into *Brian's Song*.) Okay, maybe you think I need therapy. Well, I've had it, and it didn't help.

15. Speaking of therapy, I struggle with depression. I'm one of the few "lucky ones" whose doctor won't prescribe medication because he doesn't think the depression is bad enough. This is how it goes. I go to see Dr. Beuter and tell him I'm feeling very depressed lately and am wondering if medication would help. He tells me I don't really show signs of "severe" depression, that I would be much more despondent if I were truly clinically depressed. Why can't he be one of those drug-happy doctors who medicates anyone for anything? How did I end up with Dr. Clean? Next visit, I'm thinking about getting into the fetal position and quacking like a duck in the corner of the examining room just so I can get the stuff. If he wants "despondent," I'll give it to him.

16. I'm too self-conscious. I wonder if I'll ever be as secure as those people who have the guts to eat dinner alone in a

restaurant or go see a movie by themselves. If running on a treadmill, I'll glance over to see the speed level of the guy next to me. Maybe I'm just imagining it, but it seems every time I increase my speed, he one-ups me.

17. I've done my share of things in adult life that fall in the you-do-what-you-have-to-do-to-get-by category: selling carpet, cleaning up construction sites, washing dishes, and restocking department store shelves. I am convinced everyone should work retail at least once to really understand the world in which we live. I tend to distrust people who claim to speak for God unless I know they have waited tables when shorthanded or operated a cash register during an early-bird special. You can spend a lot of time and money earning a degree in psychology, sociology, or anthropology, or work a few months restocking and straightening the linen section during a Wal-Mart "white sale." My specific tour of duty was at Kohl's department store, where I was awarded "Employee of the Month" my first month. I finally left in fear of committing homicide in the rug aisle on one of those insidious customers who insist on unfolding the rugs before buying one and leave the unwanted ones all over the floor, walking away without a thought.

Why am I telling you all this? I just want you to know up front that I am a very ordinary (probably subordinary) person. I am not wealthy, famous, or brilliant (I might not even be stable). I have not accomplished anything spectacular or won any great victory for humanity, and many things I hoped and dreamed for in life have not materialized. Yet these past few years I've been stumbling into questions that seem to be leading somewhere important. What if God is actually fond of abnormal "normal" people like me, and our greatest epiphanies come while watching our kids at soccer practice or standing in line at the grocery store? What if his plan to save the world is hidden beneath the radar, behind the scenes, and among the everyday lives of nobodies? Maybe the epic story of God redeeming the world is more Frodo- and Sam-like than we think. Could God have placed the fate of his created realm in the hands of flawed, neurotic, Windows 98 kinds of people? Scary, isn't it?

I pretty much graduated high school, college, and seminary by the skin of my teeth, but I think I'm on to something here. At the risk of sounding too Da Vinci Code–ish, I'm beginning to see how the secret ways and deepest mysteries of God and his kingdom are often revealed off the beaten path of organized religion and frequently missed by the too-smart. Sometimes it's not the professor or preacher leading you to divine truth but the commonplace people God sticks right in front of your face. The Bible says something about "jars of clay" being fit vessels for carrying eternal treasure and God using "foolish," "weak," "lowly," "despised" people in profound ways (see 2 Corinthians 4:7; 1 Corinthians 1:27–28). A wonderful freedom is growing inside me knowing there's hope, meaning, and purpose for unimpressive people like me. Maybe God supplies everything I need, and my part is believing, trusting, and depending. I have my reasons for believing all these things, which you will see.

I never felt as if I measured up to or fit in with people who seemed to be professionals in the field of God, even though I tried hard to be one of them. Both as a leader and rank-and-file member, I became disillusioned with institutional church and contemplated chucking Christianity but discovered they were two separate and not nearly equal things. I remember often thinking to myself, *There's got to be more to it than this*. I'm discovering there is. This journey has cost me, sometimes dearly. One should try to avoid upsetting the religious crowd if at all possible, and things get downright ugly when drilling down to the darkest truths about yourself.

Okay, enough of all that. If I go on too long like this, I may need to go visit Dr. Beuter again and insist that he hand over the Prozac. Let's just end with this: If I haven't scared you off by now with the vision of me sitting in an old recliner in my garage watching *Mr. Holland's Opus* on my little fuzzy-screen TV, fighting off the tears, then you may actually get something out of the rest of this. But I'm not promising anything.

Real Introduction

THE "NOVEL" (READ "PERSONAL MEMOIR") I'VE BEEN WORK-
ING on for several years is titled *The Unraveling: How Jamie
Blue Made His Peace and Almost Lived to Tell About It*.
Jamie Blue is the central character of a saga revolving around
religion's failure to rescue him from a horrific childhood and,
in the end, how religion almost destroyed him.

Here's an excerpt using fictional names to fit my novel but
describing the nonfiction realities of my childhood:

> *If the walls of my childhood home could speak, they would tell*
> *the sad story of a woman ensnared in the depths of despair*
> *and a little boy who hated himself for failing to free her. Mom*
> *would tell me I was her only reason for living. Two hours later*
> *I would be pleading with her not to kill herself or run away*
> *from home. Before I knew multiplication tables, Mother relied*
> *on me as her counselor. Before my first date, she depended on*
> *me as she would a husband. Although a large crucifix of Jesus*
> *hung on the living room wall, she clung to me as her savior.*
>
> *Mother dragged a heavy sack behind her filled with a life-*
> *time of pain and sorrow. She often knelt before me, recount-*
> *ing events of her tragedy-laced life, including the early death*

of her alcoholic father, the tragic loss of her first child, and the passing away of her marriage to my father. She would lay her depraved memories at my feet, begging me to take them all away. I never said anything in those moments, but as seconds gave way to years, that terrified little boy was dying in the silence.

When I was six years old, my father plotted in secret to have Mother committed to an insane asylum. After his failed attempt, she trusted no one and lived in the mental prison of paranoia, both on the inside and outside of psychiatric hospitals, through the years. One day my sister called me for the first time since I left home, suspecting Mother might be dead because she wasn't answering her phone. I told her to call 911, packed a gym bag with a few clothes, and broke the speed limit across three states to get home. When I arrived at Bedford County Hospital, the doctor told me paramedics kicked in the door of her small apartment on Harding Road across from the cemetery. They found her passed out on the floor of the bedroom, a lit cigarette smoldering in an ashtray on her bed, and a blood alcohol content so high she should have been dead.

They put my mother in a hospital room with a curtain dividing her and an elderly man with sweat pouring down his face as he twisted and turned in wrangled sheets while hallucinating with ghostly groans. Carefully slipping the curtain back, horror and heartbreak filled my eyes. She lay with her back toward me, curled into a ball of shivering bones, and her head of snarled white hair turned to the hospital window. I was powerless to move as tears slowly trickled down my cheeks, giving rise to streams of sadness for this woman crumbling under the weight of sixty-some years of heartbreak and suffering.

Forcing down emotion, I cautiously eased closer. When sensing my presence, she turned her head toward the ceiling, *catching me out of the corner of her eye. She fought one limb at a time to position her ninety-pound wiry body flat on the bed. Her effort is culminated in a sigh of exhaustion as she fixed her vacant eyes on mine. With a lost look in her skeletal face, she said nothing. Raising her trembling hand full of arthritic knots, she rested it on the top of my hand, now tightly wrapped around the cold metal guardrail on the side of her bed. It's unsettling how one moment in time can carry the collective force of all painful moments preceding it. That is what I experienced when our eyes met only briefly, for I could not bare gazing too deeply. She grimaced as her eyes closed and wept dry tears of shame, for her dehydrated body had not a drop to waste.*

Like every good alcoholic, she hid bottles behind stacks of magazines in the closet and buried them beneath sweaters, claiming hangovers were migraine headaches. She drank heaviest when I was at school and was often passed out on the couch when I got home. Named Margaret Anne, she was the middle daughter of three Dunning girls raised in Marion, Virginia, on meager means by my iron-willed and widowed grandmother during the Great Depression. She married my father, Jon Joseph Blue, with child in June of 1953 and gave birth that November, naming her firstborn Clara May. Meningitis took my natural sister's life just short of her sixth birthday. The resulting desperation drove Mother to abruptly adopt a son and two daughters. Five years later (1964), I came to be as an unplanned intrusion. She was a single mother of two sons and two daughters and often cried while folding clothes and washing dishes.

She never spoke of the premature deaths of her father and first child but often ventured down to the basement where she kept their photographs and other keepsakes locked in a wooden trunk. When grief called her down there in the middle of the night, I remember burying my head beneath pillows to muffle the sobs and screams of her tortured spirit. She learned from her father that alcohol brought only temporary relief and escape from what ails you. There was no bottle deep enough to bury Mother's pain.

People said she was crazy because she talked of hearing voices. I wonder if those voices spoke to her in the hospital room that day, and I wonder what they said. Perhaps she heard her father cursing in fits of drunken rage, or years later her absentminded mother rambling in the Alzheimer's ward of a nursing home, or the voice of her baby girl crying out from her early grave. I never took her hand, fearing the heartache of what we never had would be the final blow that killed her, but I did plead with God in my heart to take the voices away. Inside me I carry very deep and almost overpowering sadness for my mother. I imagine her as the little blonde-haired girl she once was, with all the hopes and dreams little blonde-haired girls have. When I think of all these things, my heart is truly broken, and I will carry that brokenness with me to the very end.

My reason for becoming a Christian the summer after barely graduating high school was to escape hell—two of them actually. One, I was told, lost people suffer in after death; the other was the first eighteen years of my life. Being an unwanted child, failing to rescue my mom from her misery, and abandoned by my father, I have always felt the burden of proof squarely upon my shoulders to prove I have a right to exist. I was looking to purge that part of my life and found abundant metaphorical support in Christianity, where one is "born again" and "the old is gone and the new has come."

In college, I immediately connected with Christian groups that offered more than enough opportunity to cover up the pain of my childhood wounds with meetings, programs, and activities. I was mesmerized in Christian conferences by slogans such as "Come help change the world," "The time is now," and "Leave a mark no one can erase." I couldn't save my mom, but with God I had a new mission to save the world. Perhaps I wasn't so worthless after all. Growing into adulthood, I lacked the raw materials needed to fashion a creditable identity. I wasn't smart or gifted, and there was virtually nothing I seemed good at. Then one day at my university I was asked to speak in front of a group of fellow students and managed to preach an impassioned sermon, said by some to border on the equivalent of MLK's "I have a dream" speech, and was hailed savior (student president) of our campus ministry. Afterward, folks said I was a natural leader because I motivated (er . . . manipulated) people toward committed involvement.

The Christian thing was going well. Like Jesus, I began in humble circumstances, but unlike him, I rode high on the palm branches of people's praise. I'm sure that was where my addiction to becoming a mega-something (anything) was born. On the first day of classes, a professor looked at my official name on his roll, called out "James Patrick Palmer," and, assuming as much, asked if I went by Jim. Up to that point, I had always been called Jamie, and to this day it is the name I am known by in Blacksburg. I was pleased to accept the name change, which made my transformation complete. Jamie Palmer was buried, and Jim Palmer was born.

For the next fifteen years, I never looked back and poured my soul into Christian ministry. I earned a master of divinity, landed my first ministry position at the largest, most innovative church in North America, and received front-page newspaper coverage in the city upon launching my very own first church. I was well on my way to becoming one of those Christian gurus who are invited to pontificate at seminars and conventions. This Christian thing was reeeeeeally going well, and I could not have scripted a better zero-to-hero scenario to prove I wasn't the worthless nobody the place deep down inside me still ardently claimed.

Of course, at the time, I was not consciously aware of all these motivations. I was simply a man on a mission from God. I also do not consider the things I did all for naught. At any given moment, each of us is a mixed bag of motives, the known and the unknown. In the end, God understands we all are pretty messed up but not outside the realm of his ability to save. I was convinced God wanted (even needed) me for the mission of saving the world (again, I needed some mission to justify taking up space on planet Earth), when all along God mostly wanted to save me—not just the get-out-of-hell-free kind of salvation, but the setting-me-free-from-the-crap kind. So there I was, flailing about in the ocean of my despair, while still insistent on trying to rescue others. I had experienced enough significant failures to cause a normal person to look deep within, but I wasn't and am not normal. Other than Jacob in the Old Testament, I might be the only other person stubborn enough to wrestle with God and actually have a legitimate shot at winning.

Turns out, God has his ways. Thankfully, on this journey God has provided the necessary epiphanies to save me from complete self-destruction and has opened my eyes to deeper realities. With a seminary degree under my belt, you would think those epiphanies would have come when caught up in a deep theological treatise—Calvin's *Institutes*, perhaps, or Barth's *Ethics*. But that's not what happened. What happened is what I've attempted to peck out (I can't type worth a flip) in the following pages. God opened my eyes, not through theological and philosophical flashes of brilliance, but through the unlikeliest people—people I, well, just kind of ran into along the way. Everyday run-of-the-mill types, like you and me. The cast of characters includes a Waffle House waitress, a tire salesman, a hiphop artist, and a swim teacher, among others. Each of them unraveled a bit more the mystery of God and stretched the capacity of my soul to know him. Once my eyes were opened to this, it was like I was born again . . . again.

On one of my long runs (that's any distance beyond three blocks), it dawned on me that perhaps God's reason for wanting me is much better than my reason for wanting him. Maybe God's idea of my salvation trumps the version I am too willing to settle for. Uncovering your true reasons for wanting God and learning God's real purpose for wanting you are a couple of revelations you need to have in order to get down heaven's road. The first requires a brutal self-honesty, and the second an elastic head and heart, both of which you sometimes need a little help acquiring.

The people and places my help comes from border on the bizarre. I've been down quite a few spiritual detours and rabbit holes that somehow ended up at places I needed to visit. Sometimes the "detours" were actually paths toward greater enlightenment, and the ones I presumed right were the real detours headed nowhere. Let's just say I have learned to keep my eyes wide open. I must tell you, I am not a proponent of "religion," even the "Christian" kind, but have never gone wrong following Jesus. Yes, I know it all sounds absurd. To really understand, you need to step into my shoes and follow your feet.

one

Touched by a Drummer (Saint Kit)

Knowing God

Warning: *The journey ahead assumes you've read the two introductions. Skipping them could lead to the end of life on this planet as we know it. You wouldn't want that hanging over your head, would you?*

HOW DO YOU EXPLAIN A STRONG PREMONITION PULLING you toward an unknown place to meet someone you don't know? Oddly enough, I was always just one person away from Saint Kit, but it took a midlife collapse to bring us face-to-face. The summit of significance was finally in view after years of maneuvering the challenges of leadership in Christian ministry. With one final push to the top left to go, an unexpected snowstorm blew in, and I was forced to abort the mission. In a matter of moments, my ascent to greatness became a brutal struggle to survive. It was clear I wasn't going to safely get off that mountain without some help.

From Nashville, I landed in New Haven late Friday afternoon, driving a two-lane highway all the way to West Simsbury. A light dusting of snow covered the roadside, with silvery flakes continuing to drop gently from the dusk-filled sky. Following

1

directions, I veered right at the fork and continued crawling along, finding my left turn past an old, round, stone barn. A meandering gravel driveway led through spacious, pine-covered land to an old New England farmhouse. The scent of burning wood accompanied a coal-black Labrador announcing my arrival, both tail and tongue vigorously engaged.

Contrasting the external magnificence of the Connecticut surroundings was the hemorrhaging man behind the wheel. My zero-to-hero story, the one where I take my place between Frodo and Sam to be counted among the fellowship of "somebodies" winning great victories for humankind (or at least invited to speak at a church-growth conference), wasn't quite going as planned. On the brink of reaching coveted guru status, I discovered my wife of ten years had entered into a relationship with another man. This revelation sent our marriage plummeting, and after failed attempts in counseling to save it, it ended in divorce. Other than the consolation of having no children of our own to put through the nightmare of a broken marriage, I could not imagine any scenario where this could "work out for the good." At first I tried dodging any personal responsibility and strived to save face by emphasizing the technicality that *she* was the one who filed for divorce, but ultimately I could not escape the cruel truth that our marriage failed in part because *I* failed.

Soon after, I resigned as pastor of the church I'd started, which was widely known, having once been a Sunday morning front-page story in the city paper. In the dead of winter, I packed my belongings and moved in with a single guy from our church, living in an ancient house without heat. News traveled fast and far, reaching the mega mother church up north where I'd been trained and commissioned.

Becoming a marked man is an abrupt and rude awakening

for someone on the rise toward greatness. No explanation sufficed, and any way you sliced it, folks saw a promising ministry star who had crashed and burned. You can get away with quite a bit in career Christendom, but divorce is on the taboo black list of ultimate no-no's. Stripped of my superhero-minister mask and exposed as a mere mortal, I became unnecessary among people who once hung on my every word.

I surmised heaven had me marked too, no longer just a child of God, but now a divorced one. My sense of value and usefulness crashed, and I shamefully assumed my place in the land of misfit toys on the outskirts of God's kingdom. At least there was the promise of Christ's return and my making it into eternal paradise, if even by the back door.

Perhaps everyone finds him or herself a time or two sifting through the rubble and ruins of a devastated life, wondering whether or not it's worth rebuilding or even salvageable. Somehow surviving the day, the night hours slowly passed in anguish as I lay awake feeling abandoned by everyone (mostly God), unable to envision a life worth living. À la Forrest Gump, one day I just started running. Dark, light, morning, afternoon, evening, rain, shine, heat, cold, seven days a week, sometimes two times a day, I strapped on my Reeboks, hit the door, and ran. I ran until my waistline and body fat dwindled to a jeans size I can only dream of now. At first it was three miles, then five miles, then nine, then twelve, seventen, twenty-two, until one day I collapsed, unconscious, and awoke inside an ambulance.

Eventually realizing I couldn't outrun my problems, I began paying a counselor more than I could afford to sit and listen to my rambling for an hour. It was money well spent, since no one else cared to hear what I needed to say. My shrink mentioned hearing about some guy in Connecticut who provided a place

3

for people to get away by themselves for rest and to "listen to God." It was worth a shot. I was doing plenty of blathering; maybe it was time for listening. So I called this dude in Connecticut, and after an hour of spilling my guts, I decided to go. Maybe he would have some answers (or a magic wand) to piece my shattered life back together.

It was a little odd on the phone. All he wanted to talk about was "silence," "solitude," and "meditation." I began envisioning Kit as one of those yoga fanatics or some gaunt monastic sage wandering the countryside in a robe and sandals, feeding birds and chipmunks or making fruitcakes by candlelight while chanting and burning incense. Neither was I sure my psyche could handle being that far north while Atlanta faced New York in the World Series. How could a red-state Bible Belt Baptist Braves fan possibly fraternize with a blue-state Catholic Yankees fanatic? Isn't that sleeping with the enemy? Nonetheless, desperate times called for desperate measures, so off I went.

So here I was in Connecticut, and at the end of that long driveway, a burly man in grungy jeans and a rust-colored sweater appeared on the front steps waving me in, an ecstatic grin on his face. Bypassing my outstretched hand, he embraced me solidly, paralyzing me. I am not a touchy-feely kind of guy. This was Kit? He sure didn't resemble the solemn monks in my church history books. He grabbed my bags and ushered me inside to the savory smell of chow and his lovely wife, Trish.

Over dinner it became clear that Kit wasn't the friar I expected. A gifted jazz drummer, music is his passion and genius. In addition to playing and listening to it, he somehow introduced the topic into most conversations. He would mention names of renowned musicians, and I would nod my head as if I knew whom he was talking about. At some point, I was going to have to break it to him that my music tastes weren't quite so sophisticated. He hadn't said anything yet about Alabama or Hootie and the Blowfish. We did have a chat later about Genesis—not the Bible one, but the Phil Collins one.

Physically unassuming, Kit has a quietly calm presence that mysteriously draws you. He comes to mind as what must be meant when people refer to someone as being "centered." He listened twice as much as he spoke, which worked well since I talked twice as much as I listened. It wasn't long before I realized Kit had no intention of offering advice or counseling me on the trauma precipitating my pilgrimage to see him. Some sage! To him, nature provided a breathtaking backdrop, and they supplied a bed, three square meals, and quiet, and it was up to God to do the rest. He and Trish lived upstairs in the retreat house they made available to people worn down and weary, or somehow lost due north. My being there was starting to make more sense—maybe there was something more to this God thing than I had experienced thus far.

Speaking of God, reading between the lines, it seemed Kit had this silly notion that God just talks to people. To him, "prayer" was a kind of real-time instant-messaging soul conversation with God. It figures that a freewheeling, inventive musician type would come up with something so right-brained as that. Didn't Kit know the Bible made all that unnecessary? God has already spoken, his love letter to all of humankind is in print, there is nothing left to say, and those claiming to hear God "speak" are usually cult leaders stockpiling weapons and planning their own armageddon.

I was tired, and Kit showed me the sleeping quarters. Surrounded by silent wintry woods, a wall of windows clothed in sheer curtains let moonlight wash over the entire room. Lingering at the window, I watched the snowflakes float effortlessly around bare branches reaching quietly toward the light. I finally pulled myself away from the window and closed my bedroom door, making sure it was securely locked. The safety of a locked door helped me sleep as a child and was comforting in unfamiliar places. I slipped into bed, pulled up the extra blanket, and swiftly drifted off.

The clock read 2:00 a.m. when I was sharply roused from the dead of sleep. Sitting up on the side of my bed, I carefully surveyed the softly lit room and was startled to find my locked bedroom door now standing half open. Someone was there. I could feel it. What words can be used to describe what is beyond speech? The next moment I was swept away by the awareness of a vast and powerful presence before me. At first I was anxious before its immensity, yet just an instant later, I was delighting in its beauty and love. It was like I had been opened from within, and in the depths of my being, an indescribable joy, a kind of gusto, filled me and set me afloat on a sea of happiness so freeing and complete that it remains in my memory to this day as perfect peace.

A glowing intimacy such as I had never felt before was turned upon me, and finite language cannot express the intoxicating pleasure I felt as emanating waves of tender affection washed over me. I responded by accepting it, even more, wanting it. Whoever or whatever this was I did not care, glad to leave behind everything in life that was less than this. Slowly swaying back and forth, basking in the ecstasy and rapture of this encounter, I closed my eyes and began patting my heart. There was nothing to think, say, or do, so totally was I caught up in receiving. Completely absorbed in the fullness and significance of the moment, it was like the clouds of my soul had parted and warm rays of divine love were streaming in. Lingering in delight, a sweet drowsiness slowly began claiming me, which I first fought, not wanting to let go of the moment. The last thing I remember was snowflakes quietly and more steadily dropping outside the window before falling back off to sleep.

(Okay, the last few paragraphs sound like something out of one of those sappy paperback romance novels with Joe Stud passionately embracing little Miss Helpless on the cover. I almost didn't include this section, imagining the horrified faces of my gym buddies reading it. Guys, if you're reading this, how 'bout those White Sox!)

I'm not a big paranormal kind of guy, though I once saw what looked like a UFO flying over my apartment building, but I promised Pam not to get into that here. (Yet another publishing world insight: The real editor is your spouse, who must continue living with you after the book comes out.) Based on the nighttime visitation, I was half expecting to find Kit levitating over his music gear with drumsticks in hand at the breakfast table. What kind of music was this guy into (or smoking while listening)? Whatever my encounter was, it certainly was a leap attributing this craziness to God, at least the Judeo-Christian one I knew. He was still packed in my bag between Genesis and Revelation.

Like summoning a genie in a bottle, I was familiar with summoning God for life application through proper inductive Bible study methods. I wasn't well acquainted with the one who shows up bedside like your lover. Though my New Age friends spoke of being in deep accord with a "quantum essence," my Christian spirituality didn't leave room for knowing God so intimately, so personally. I learned all about God's "omnipresence" in seminary and didn't need to "feel" God to know that he was with me. My faith was much more sophisticated.

Over breakfast, Kit sat listening for the better part of an

hour to my sharing what seemed the most relevant facts of my life story. Navigating like a brain surgeon around people and circumstances dangerously near tender scars, I suddenly fell speechless upon accidentally puncturing a painful wound and could not continue. Not quick to intervene, Kit offered a concerned smile and after a long, uncomfortable silence said, "Perhaps it's time for quiet." In the stillness, there was no escaping my brokenness. Perhaps this was why solitude was so threatening. With the noise of my frenetic activity silenced, the muffled voices of emptiness and despair then demanded to be heard.

As conversation resumed, he asked me to describe where I was with God. Rambling off a heap of words, it sure didn't seem to be adding up to much. I was a born-again, inerrancy-defending, seeker-targeted pastor, steamrolled by life, trying to figure out, What now? After a moment or two of wallowing in my woes, he responded with, "Jim, could you describe what you know of God?" An inner sigh of relief (like the classroom discovery of knowing the right answer) came, remembering all I knew about God. God is eternal, infinite, holy, just, sovereign, wise, atemporal, omniscient, omnipresent, all-powerful, majestic, unchanging, merciful, and loving. I had a few Gospel stories about Jesus to back it up, a couple of examples of how God "blessed" me, and I expected to earn extra credit upon citing the beauty of the New England winter as proof of virtually every attribute of God.

Kit was unmoved by my theological competence. He rephrased his request this time by emphasizing, "Jim, describe what you know of God *from personal experience.*" He clarified this further by saying, "Jim, how would you answer the question, 'Who is God?' if you could not use any information you've learned about God from the Bible? Describe for me who you have experienced God to be through your personal interaction with him." Yikes! *When's the soonest flight back to Nashville?* I wondered. Every good evangelical knows that for all practical purposes, the Bible *is* God, and you don't rely on something as subjective as personal experience. Heck, I knew people who slept with their Bible beneath their pillow to keep God close. Perhaps Kit should stick to playing drums and leave religion to trained professionals.

Seeing I was getting a bit fidgety and defensive, Kit suggested spending the rest of the afternoon in quiet "listening." For what, I didn't know. Expecting Kit's guidance for determining my next move in life, I was now going to blow an entire day listening to birds chirp. I bundled up, grabbed a notebook and a pen, and we headed out into the frigid Connecticut winter. Kit led me along a wooded trail to an old dairy barn and escorted me upstairs to the hayloft, which had been converted into a sitting room. Pulling from his pocket a box of matches, he lit the single candle on a small wooden table, motioning me to take a seat.

Kit stood gazing out the window while I watched the small flame in the middle of the room. A few moments had passed when he began speaking to God on my behalf as if I weren't even there. Appealing to Jesus for my worn-out soul to find rest in him, he was seeing more deeply into my need than I could see myself. Maybe he knew something I didn't. I went to Connecticut expecting a list of things to do in order to get my life back on track but, come to think of it, Kit had not asked one thing of me since arriving. He and Trish provided for my every practical need and wouldn't even let me pour my own coffee refill. Was there a message in this? I came to Connecticut anxiously seeking answers, direction, and an action plan, and felt an elephant-sized burden of successfully obtaining at least one; but the more the merrier, right? Maybe instead I was there to receive, and the burden was really on God to provide whatever I needed. Perhaps that is what Kit meant by listening—an openness to receiving.

Kit remained a short while longer and indicated he'd be back to get whatever was left of me before sundown. The barn door creaked shut behind him as I sat listening to the slowly fading cadence of his footsteps in the snow. The steady flame of the candle kindled a heightened attentiveness, and I deciphered the sound of beads of water dripping outside from overhead icicles onto the front steps. A whistling winter wind gently rattled the windowpanes. Some distance away I could make out the sound of firewood being split and farther away still, the faint whistle of a train. It's amazing what you hear when you're listening.

My mind set to wandering in the quiet, and I found myself lost in memories as a young boy drawing pictures. There I was ripping pencil sketches and paintings, which had taken hours to create, into shreds. Despite the praise of elementary school teacher Miss Scott after once catching a glimpse of my artistic doodling, my eyes could see only flaws and defects in every work I created. With wadded-up paper piled across my bedroom floor, I would berate myself for the ugliness of my pictures. Now all grown up and sitting atop this barn in Connecticut, my self-hatred seemed to have come full circle. Born again as a high school senior, I had been supplied by God with a fresh start and a clean page for creating a new life, but I had managed to turn it into a horrid splattering of dark blotches. Tears of shame trickled down my cheeks to the corners of my mouth, where I could taste the regretful reality that after all these years, the only picture I had to present to God seemed to be ugly and worthless.

As I sat in silence at the rock bottom of myself, I noticed the candle suddenly flicker and immediately felt a peculiar stirring as if something had been altered within myself or in the room or both. A finely tuned attentiveness grew. I spoke into the silence, "Is that you, Jesus?" Where did that thought come from? The deeper I sank into my inner desolation, the stronger this presence became. Could this really be Jesus? Why? How? Where was Kit when you needed him? My brain finally conceded to what my soul unmistakably knew; the risen Christ was knocking at the door of my broken heart with something to say.

I opened my notebook and began writing out an unfolding conversation between Jesus and myself. Addressing me personally by name, he initiated his thoughts into my mind, which I recorded and then responded to in writing. I continued in this manner, filling several pages. The first brief exchange opened the eyes of my heart to see Jesus as never before and then myself through his eyes:

"Jim, the man I deeply love, may I come in? I want to be with you. You have not been hidden from me. I look upon you now in sadness; the one I love is broken."

"Jesus, who am I?"

"Jim, I see that little boy and now grown man ashamed of his picture. When I came to you last night, I hurt over your disconnectedness and loneliness. These very sorrows I have felt myself. I was unwanted and undesirable. I know your lonely place. Jim, you are desired and wanted by me. You condemn yourself, but I want you to be free."

"I am so tired, Jesus. My whole life is a failure."

"I take great delight in you, Jim. I want you to know that and rest in it. I look upon the picture of your life and smile.

I know you now, who you are in the process of becoming day by day, and ultimately who you will fully be. I rejoice over you with singing."

Perhaps the unknown man I was drawn to Connecticut to meet wasn't Kit after all, but Jesus. Apparently, I had not mastered knowing God as my master of divinity degree implied. I prided myself in knowing what the Bible said *about* God, but I now was experiencing an aspect of encountering him directly. Putting two and two together, I realized it was Jesus pursuing me at my bedside as my smitten lover. He was letting me know that I am his greatest treasure and that he is determined for me to know this about myself.

The combination of the bedroom encounter and now this chat with God, especially given my UFO sighting, might raise suspicions with the reader of my having a shaky hold on reality. I feel your pain. Perhaps others imagine I've seen one too many episodes of *Joan of Arcadia*. To be honest, I probably could have passed the whole thing off as some psychological castle in the sky if it weren't for this one thing—the conversation is continuing. Jesus keeps on talking. Or is it that I've finally started listening?

For years of my life, my approach to God was akin to the field of astronomy. God was this immense celestial phenomenon, and the Bible was my telescope through which I caught distant glimpses, recording my observations, calculations, and interpretations in Sunday school guides and fill-in-the-blank sermon notes. My understanding of how things worked was that an accurate knowledge of the composition of God and the spiritual laws for relating to him was the difference between being blessed or blighted by this divine juggernaut. With a seminary degree and a lifetime of studying the Bible, I was considered an expert on God, and people drove from miles away to hear me explain him. Kit was instrumental in opening my eyes to the fact that God wants me to *know* him in a way beyond how you know French or geometry (curious choice, since I don't know French and failed geometry, but you get the point).

Admittedly, my purely intellectual approach to God was inconsistent with my evangelical jargon that often referred to a "personal relationship" with God. I had the rhetoric down but did not really experience God this way in everyday life. I did have a sort of relationship with my Bible, as much as one can have a relationship with a book. I had a wide range of motivations for making the Bible the center of my life. Sometimes I read the Bible because it was drilled into me that I should, a God-won't-like-me-if-I-don't kind of should. At other times, I came to the Bible as God's little instruction book for improving my life and fixing my problems. I searched the Scriptures for promises to claim and principles to apply in achieving a successful life (including financial independence, vocational achievement, and cured depression). Reading the Bible was also a checklist item I could easily mark off in order to feel good about myself, kind of like exercising daily and taking my vitamins.

Referring to the Bible, Jesus once said, "These Scriptures point to me." Pondering Jesus's words, I was a little startled by the implication that the written Word and the Living Word are not one and the same. On one level, this is patently obvious. When Jesus returns, he will not be a book falling out of the sky. Yet, on another level, somehow I became dependent on the Bible independent of Jesus. Many world religions have sacred writings (e.g., Torah, Koran, Book of Mormon, and others), but I'm beginning to see that Christianity is centered in a Person, not a book. The written Word was given to draw us into relationship with the Living Word. Relationships revolve around the intimate interaction of two. I don't study and memorize information about my wife. Pam and I live in the same house and can relate any time and way we choose. Likewise, God dwells in me, and he is present and accessible 24/7. Now consider, if Pam is inspired to write me a love letter as part of our relationship, is her letter the totality of Pam? Will she never express those same sentiments in other ways as our relationship unfolds?

Being honest with myself, I was making the Bible God out of the need for safety and predictability. I could read any Scripture in the Bible and come back to it weeks later, and it would say the same thing. That is comforting, something solid, unchanging, controllable, and certain. Listening to and interacting with God in the moment in relational ways is messier and evokes fear. What if I fail? What if I hear wrong? What about those crazies who claim God "told them" to commit murder or the guy who believes God said to change jobs and it all falls apart? But aren't all relationships like this, exposing us to risk and vulnerability? Can growing, vibrant relationships be predictable and controllable, and aren't they a process of trial and error as we get to know the other? Maybe knowing God is less a science and more an art.

Kit's love for music finds expression through several avenues, including concerts, recording projects, and teaching. During one of our conversations, Kit explained to me that as a musician he is trained to improvise and doesn't fear the moment. I experienced this firsthand in the way he responded during my visit. With no preplanned agenda, he improvised with the Holy Spirit as he observed what God was doing with me. Both within his music and within his relationship with God, he has learned there are wonders to explore if you can live in the existing tension, mystery, and unpredictability.

Now I knew why I had to visit Kit. God put me with someone who had enough confidence in the Spirit to let my visit play out as God directed. I've received a lot of "ministry training" from some of the best and brightest megastars in Christendom, but I learned my most valuable lesson from Kit: Sometimes it's just best to get out of God's way. Plenty of people were willing to offer "biblical counsel" concerning my continuing career and ministry, which would have served only as distractions from listening to and knowing God himself up close and personal in real time. I was one of those people Jesus referred to who had their nose buried in the written Word but somehow missed the Living Word. Arriving in Connecticut, I wanted a five-point plan for putting my life back together, but Kit's unplanned agenda allowed for moments where I experienced God in ways I never had.

Maybe getting there requires coming to the end of yourself and the things and people you're depending on, even if they are inherently good, like the Bible. My striving couldn't get me any closer to knowing God. He had always been there, waiting for me to give up and listen. Though those dramatic encounters don't happen every day, I'm starting to become more familiar with his voice. In all Kit's improvising, I got a taste of God, making me hungry for more of him. *He* is what I'm looking for. The risks are worth it. I can't control or predict God, but I trust him enough to allow this journey of knowing him to take me wherever it may lead, even if I don't know where that is until I get there.

Guess that's like marching to the beat of a different drummer, huh?

two

Hip-Hop Geography
(Extreme Doug)

Straight Up

MY FRIEND DOUG KNOWS JESUS AND BELIEVES EMINEM is a musical genius with something to say worth listening to. This is disturbing to many people who feel something has desperately gone wrong in a world where the names Eminem and Jesus could even be in the same sentence. For those of you who don't know who Eminem is, that might be best. This chapter will be less troubling by not knowing. If you must know and you have teenagers, just ask them. Either way, I can't be responsible for what you find Googling his name on the Internet.

They say you can tell a lot about a person based on their car. You would learn the following things about Doug by snooping around his worn and rusty van, which I secretly did once when he went back into a restaurant for his missing cell phone (I credit my investigative skills to watching many episodes of *CSI*):

- He's a Minnesota Vikings fan (notice the bumper sticker and purple van).

- He eats beef jerky (discover wrappers crammed into glove compartment).

- He's a craftsman (see piles of tools and containers of glop).

- He's into martial arts (imagine gym bags stuffed with uniform and gear).

- He likes hip-hop music (check the CD collection with parental-advisory labels).

Growing up in a musically talented family, Doug evolved into a classically trained percussionist and later an accomplished symphony player. He morphed into the "go-to drummer for-hire" on the Chicago and Milwaukee nightclub scene for jazz and progressive rock bands. Though he is still recognized as an exceptional percussionist, he now only plays for fun and occasional favors. He takes time to help out promising up-and-comers, including hard-core rockers and rappers. If he's not playing with them, he's listening to and supporting them in local clubs and bars. In recent years, Doug has particularly become immersed in hip-hop. (**Hip-hop n.: 1.** an American cultural movement primarily composed of break dancing, graffiti art, and what is known as hip-hop music, which combines rapping (emceeing) and deejaying in a variety of styles. **2.** A booty-dancing, gangsta-glorifying, establishment-dissing assault on Western civilization.)

If you just get to know Doug in everyday life, you experience him to be an easygoing, lay-low kind of person. Nonjudgmental and accepting, Doug is the person you first think of to call when your car or marriage breaks down. He is fun loving and good humored and the guy you want bringing the ball up the court (great point guard).

I was conflicted about Doug, because until I uncovered Eminem, Ludicris, and Dr. Dre CDs in his van, I had no idea that he was, well, you know . . . one of them. He seemed fairly normal, but I wondered when the nice-guy facade would give way to the real Doug. Come on, anyone can see on MTV that hip-hop is basically one big orgy of sexual license and trigger-happy rage wrapped in lewd language and masquerading as music and art. Sure, I prayed for these poor lost souls on their fast track to hell, but I had never really known one.

It really blew my mind when I eventually discovered the following other things about Doug:

- He is not a crazed sex fiend (Doug is happily married with three children).
- He has no criminal record and doesn't hate cops.
- He doesn't use the "f-word" (occasionally the "s-word" when the hammer misses).
- He doesn't wake up angry every morning.
- He doesn't do drugs or sell them for extra cash.

As we began hanging out, I pieced together more of his story. Somewhere along the city street nightclubs and bars of Chicago, Doug got tired. The kind of tired that happens when your inner self jumps off the merry-go-round of existence and observes just how empty and pointless life has become. Not a "don't want to" tired, but the "can't anymore" kind. Though he was giving expression to this ache through his music, it was only becoming more unbearable. Then one night somewhere off Division Street, Doug ran into some Jesus people who opened the eyes of his heart to God's love and spoke of a whole other dimension to life and living. It was no quirk of fate to Doug that music was instrumental in his spiritual awakening. Doug doubts he ever would have recognized his need for God if his music had not made him so acutely aware of his impoverished, restless soul.

Soon after, well-intentioned Christians who caught wind of Doug's conversion advised him to quit his secular bands, abandon the bar scene, and discontinue relations with friends who were a "bad influence." He cleaned up pretty good and continued the washing cycle by following advice discouraging him from returning phone calls to his old buddies, and by trashing all his "worldly" music. Promptly, he was introduced to contemporary Christian music and asked to play in the church worship band.

It wasn't long before Doug became deeply unsettled. The gifted professional musician part of him was alarmed by the lack of originality and quality of the "Christian" music he was given and asked to play. (Doug's exact words were "Are you kidding me?" and "You can't be serious.") It felt to him like a cheap imitation. Though he trashed his CD collection, eventually he launched covert operations, slipping out to Wal-Mart on the edge of town under the cover of darkness to purchase the sinful stuff. He would rush home, pull the blinds, lock his door and windows, crank his tunes on earphones, and then hide it all in the bottom of his laundry basket when the Bible study group met at his apartment. It was a close call once when someone popped open his CD player to put in some praise music and removed a Limp Bizkit disc without noticing.

Doug soon discovered other troubling things about the God music he was now playing. The messages in the music didn't seem quite right. He quickly learned that his new friends classified music as Christian if it contained frequent references to Jesus or faith and was void of profanity. As Doug listened a little more closely, he began noticing it smacked of a "don't worry, be happy" theme with a God twist. At least his "secular" music had a certain honesty about the crap of life and desperations of the soul. This Christian music seemed shallow, simplistic, and avoided the crap altogether; as if you shouldn't have any if you truly know Jesus. None of this made sense to Doug, whose identification with the brutal honesty and struggles of his pre-Jesus music was part of what led him to God in the first place.

In addition to playing drums in the church worship band, Doug was now being asked to tour with some big-name Christian rock bands. He began witnessing disturbing disconnects between the performances, whether a Sunday worship gig or a Christian concert, and real life. Despite the upbeat vibe of morning worship and the strong Christian image presented in concerts, signs of spiritual life off stage were few and far between. Many of the players were hurting and falling apart personally, but the "show must go on" mentality took precedence, and as long as you were a church member and signed off on the agreement to abstain from alcohol, to attend rehearsals, and to wear appropriate attire on stage, all was well.

Meanwhile, Doug began running into some of his old buddies who had heard of his spiritual transformation but didn't particularly appreciate being abruptly dropped from his life. Doug was much more at home with his old friends, and soon, in addition to his clandestine Wal-Mart runs and hiding music in his laundry basket, he renewed relationships with his old buddies. Late-night conversations centered on how Jesus was deeply changing Doug's life. As his friends grew more intrigued, he invited them to his weekly Bible study group, which he immediately regretted when two guys actually decided to come.

What took Doug a while to figure out was patently obvious to his friends halfway through their first (and last) meeting. If this Jesus whom Doug spoke of was so loving and accepting, it sure hadn't rubbed off on these church people. In what they saw and heard from the leader and others in the group, Doug's newfound "spiritual relationship with God" basically came down to keeping a checklist of dos and don'ts similar to the following:

- ☐ Do go to church Sunday morning and evening and Wednesday night, and for extra credit, partake in Monday-night visitation.
- ☐ Do tithe 10 percent of your gross earnings.
- ☐ Do read your Bible a minimum of five days a week before sunrise.
- ☐ Do vote Republican.
- ☐ Do be heterosexual.
- ☐ Do evangelize, but don't fraternize with the "lost."
- ☐ Don't smoke—pipes, cigars, or cigarettes—or chew, dip, or otherwise enjoy tobacco (or alcohol).
- ☐ Don't listen to secular music.
- ☐ Don't entertain inappropriate jokes . . . except the ones that make fun of other religions or denominations.
- ☐ Don't disagree with your church pastor, elders, or staff; they know more than you do.
- ☐ Don't forget to tithe.
- ☐ Don't go back to bed when your alarm rings for predawn Bible time.

☐ Do confess sin to get right again with God if you screw up (particularly necessary for musicians who don't even know what a sunrise looks like or that five o'clock happens twice a day).

As one of his buddies put it after the last Bible studier left, "What the hell was that?" To him, the whole Jesus-thing was a load of manure that folks spread because they believed it looked nice even though it smelled like, well, you know.

The hard reality finally caught up to Doug: Although Jesus seemed capable of loving and dealing with him and his friends as they were, Christians couldn't or wouldn't. No matter how hard he tried, Doug's views and ways just didn't seem to fit in with the prevailing sensibilities of his church world. Armed with biblical proof texts, people rushed to judgment, were quick to condemn, and could not see the search for God buried beneath the behavior of people who didn't mind telling you they thought you were full of it. He discovered just because a church does contemporary music, uses media, and preaches "relevant" messages, doesn't mean they are necessarily willing to truly accept or try to understand people as they are—angry, broken, and hurting. As his Bible study leader put it once, "Doug, you are just too extreme." Hurt and disillusioned, Doug left the church (and has never gone back) and set out with Jesus on his own.

Fast-forward some years, and there I am, searching Doug's van, uncovering his music collection, and wondering if I could be arrested for some sort of crime for being a father and holding CDs displaying half-naked women and containing profanity-laden lyrics in combinations I have never heard before. Beyond the images and obscenities, Doug heard in that music a familiar message of emptiness and despair that resonated with many of the people God had placed in his life. Turns out the world needs people who deeply know Jesus and can accept and love others the way they are, even with all the junk in their lives. Perhaps many more people would be open to what Jesus offers if his followers weren't so bent on requiring you to clean up your act as a prerequisite for receiving it.

Over time, other things I had secretly uncovered (the guilt killed me, and eventually I confessed my indiscretion to Doug) in his van that day helped fill in and explain the picture of what Doug's life had become. The gym bags stuffed with martial arts gear go with him three nights a week to the tae kwon do school where Doug volunteers his time to teach inner-city youth. A fifth-degree black belt, Doug began recruiting kids from the street to use his school as an outlet for pent-up energies and to help them develop self-confidence and discipline. When Doug enters the room, you would think that God in the flesh had just strolled inside. The respect shown to Doug by the kids borders on worship. This is first because everyone knows, despite Doug's meek personality, that he could deliver a roundhouse kick in a blink that would force the question of life after death sooner than expected. The kids also show preference to Doug because they know he cares and has proved this outside of class when they needed someone to listen or intervene in a crisis. You wouldn't catch these kids dead in a church. Doug is their "church," and if he could love them the way he did, this Jesus dude couldn't be all that bad.

Martial arts master by night, Doug by day is a skilled laborer. He specializes in trim carpentry and decorative tile, which accounts for the tools and glop in the back of his van. He always seems to have enough work to have one or two guys at his side who either need a job or want to learn a trade.

Doug's choice was not to go to college, flip burgers, or sell drugs, but rather to help people learn skills like building decks and mounting tile backsplashes.

Whereas Doug's character was suspect to me because of his affinity with hip-hop, discovering I was a Christian was no less alarming to him. He knew he didn't fit with this crowd and had long since stopped trying. He held his cards close to his vest until seeing my judgmental ways were based more on ignorance than hate.

I didn't like hip-hop and Doug didn't like Christians, but we shared an obsession with Michael Jordan and the Chicago Bulls and sometimes hooked up to catch a game on WGN. One night, knowing I was uneasy with his music tastes, Doug asked if I'd be willing to watch some of an HBO show called *Def Poetry Jam*. He warned that it would contain some distasteful, offensive content and plenty of obscenities, but promised, if I paid close attention, I might experience something of "redeeming value." I began calculating how many commandments I would be breaking by watching this and if my seminary degree could be revoked if one of my professors learned of such an indiscretion. Already I had seen the half-naked women on Doug's CDs and couldn't really see how profane poetry could make it any worse, so I agreed.

Def Poetry Jam is the creation of Russell Simmons, who is commonly referred to as the godfather of the American hip-hop culture. He is credited with taking hip-hop music from the inner-city streets of New York to the shopping malls of Kansas. In addition to the music, he is said to have sold the lifestyle by mainstreaming hip-hop to urban and suburban teens. He is expected to become the first hip-hop billionaire through his empire, which consists of the Def Jam record label and a fashion line named Phat-Farm currently worth more than a half-billion dollars. (Hip-hop is a ten-billion-dollar-a-year industry.) Unlike Mr. T. and Deion Sanders, I doubt he ever appears on TBN, because he's considered by many as the driving force behind a music and culture that are poisoning the waters of America's youth.

So there I was, in fear of losing my salvation, when the first poet in dreadlocks was introduced and approached the microphone, then another . . . and another . . . and another . . . and I'm not sure exactly at what point it happened, but somewhere along the way that night something happened inside me and I've never been quite right since. Right before my eyes, pouring out their souls in prose, the obscene, obnoxious, immoral, irreligious, and enraged were unmasked for the hurting, broken, searching, fearing, confused, weary, hopeless people they (and we) are. The main difference being, they are in touch with their desperation, and we nice church people are often so out of touch.

I left Doug's place that night and decided to do a little hip-hopping of my own. I checked out a few local gigs and found the same fusion of creativity and brutal soul-searching honesty. I did research on Russell Simmons and discovered he wasn't fitting the "Satan" image I was prone to pin on him. Turns out, Russell Simmons actively opposes gang violence and believes the hip-hop culture of music, art, and dance is a nonviolent and creative outlet for hostilities. He also invests much of his own money in community development efforts and works with New York governor George Pataki (and other statewide and national political, business, sports, and entertainment leaders) to address issues such as inner-city crime, dropout rates, unemployment, and teen pregnancy. Russell Simmons understands the struggle of the street and the accompanying agony of the soul. He focuses on root issues like systemic injustice and individual responsibility, which aren't resolved by sending suburban church youth groups on "mission" trips to pick up trash, do backyard Bible studies, and hand out tracts.

I took time to learn the stories behind main players of the hip-hop scene and got to know some in my own city. Sadly, I realized just how willing I was to make judgments and level condemnation toward people who had endured an amount of suffering before age eighteen that my entire Sunday school class combined had yet to experience. We might think we have people figured out by their language, tattoos, and piercings, but I was learning the hard way we don't.

I can't go any further with this chapter until getting something off my chest with you. I wasn't born yesterday, and of course I know there are plenty of people in hip-hop who glorify sexual excess, violence, and crime to America's youth in order to make a buck. Sure, there is plenty of stupidity, toxicity, and degradation in hip-hop. The nature of any new genre of music or art begins as an authentic overflow of the soul, but eventually becomes compromised and corrupted by a glut of opportunists who jump on the moneymaking bandwagon and dilute it to the least common denominator or formula. I also know churches and church people who have imprisoned and messed up people with oppressive legalism and fear-based obedience to God in a way that hip-hop couldn't touch in its capacity to thoroughly derail and bankrupt a person's soul.

Contrary to my presumptions, Doug showed me how mistaken I was in thinking hip-hop was just about wild sex, killing cops, and selling dope. The originality of the art form and the volatile content it spews flow from the inner worlds of disillusionment, anger, and hopelessness of people who feel invisible, cast aside, rejected, and duped by their parents, politicians, and preachers who wax so eloquently about "freedom," "God," and "our way of life." As Kanye West puts it in the song "We Don't Care" on his *College Dropout* album, "Sometimes I feel no one in this world understands us, but we don't care what people say." Speaking of bandwagons, once Kanye rolled the Grammys with his megahit single "Jesus Walks," Christendom wanted to baptize him as their new superhero. I wonder what these same people would think after listening to the rest of the songs on the CD. Jack Nicholson's infamous line seems poignant here: "You can't handle the truth."

When honest, I see how conveniently I make people flaunting fleshly sins an easy target and scapegoat (and distraction from my own inner reality) as I point my finger in judgment of their immorality to feel better about myself. Despite all my spiritual rhetoric about a "relationship with God," one day I realized my Christianity was essentially a glorified behavior-modification program safely rationalized beneath a waving WWJD banner. Mostly aimed at maintaining an acceptable religious and moral exterior, at least my pharisaical front looked good in comparison to all the other "sinners" of the world who presumably were on the bottom of God's list because of their bad behavior. Maybe I need to compare myself with Snoop Dogg's filth to feel good about myself, keep the game going, and turn the spotlight off me.

Lately I've been thinking my blanket condemnation of hip-hop is really me projecting upon hiphop my own unresolved, unaccepted, unconscious desires. Somehow, somewhere along the way, my Christianity had become a hamster's squeaky wheel of dos and don'ts (which I commonly referred to as *discipleship*) that were wearing me out but not getting me anywhere. I wasn't addicted to crack; I was addicted to religion in a vain attempt to get God to like me, bless me, or at least spare me from hell when it was all over. It's funny how one can talk a good grace game, but for all practical purposes live by the law. I've learned that the "grace but . . ." mentality is as lethal as anything you can sniff, toke, or shoot up.

I was the nice, church-attending, tithing, checklist-keeping, image-projecting, good-behaving, and emotion-repressing Christian. Speaking my mind, casting off the rules, confronting the hypocrisy, upsetting the status quo, and not giving a flip what other people thought was a no-no, and it ticked me off that these hip-hoppers seemed to be getting away with it. We can rant and rave all we want, but maybe there's a little 50 Cent (megarapper) in all of us who instinctually longs for freedom and purpose but goes haywire if he doesn't find his fulfillment in God.

It's odd how we Christians are so intolerant of others' fleshly sins and so tolerant of our own so-called spiritual ones. Jesus was gentle and accepting with the adulterous woman but hammered the clerical leaders for enslaving people with religion in the name of God. Sure, people should not use their bodies sinfully because it prevents the wholeness God desires for us and others, but no less destructive are those sins not visible on a Jay-Z video that occur with all your clothes on. I discovered that pretense, duplicity, and self-righteousness are truly deadly sins, as corrupting to the soul as are excesses of the body. It's a little curious that the "sinners" in the Bible were much more responsive to Jesus and ready to receive the kingdom of God than religious people. The same sun melts wax and hardens clay, and the same Jesus melted and hardened people's hearts, but maybe there's a hidden message in who was melted (prostitutes) and who was hardened (priests).

Doesn't God want folks either passionately in love with him (hot) or flipping him the bird (cold) rather than the halfhearted mediocrity of religious compliance? Both the passion and the rebellion flow from the same source, which God placed in us and knows he must get hold of and transform (not eliminate) in order to make people whole. Many of us nice church people are sorely out of touch with this source we have rejected and long since buried beneath our religious facade.

Sure, when unplugged from God, our hardwired human impulses and instincts are unraveled into the mess people associate with Eminem. But at least those like Eminem are being honest with what they are and feel, as offensive as that may be to others. God can deal with the messy truth of who we are; he wasn't happy with the woman at the well who was prostituting her body in hopes of finding love, not just because she was doing it, but because she wouldn't admit to herself that she was. God knew this was necessary in order for her to become the whole woman he wanted her to be.

Turns out in the end, the main thing God asks of us on the road to wholeness is the truth. The idea we can "clean up our act" through our own willpower is an illusion, and the only hope of ever being whole is to receive the life of God. It's clear from the "hot/cold" Scripture in Revelation that the video nauseating God is not categorically the hip-hop one, but the one where we come to church masking our brokenness, out of touch with the truth about ourselves while pointing our fingers of condemnation at others.

The only accurate depiction of the world is a round model called a globe, because the earth itself is round. A flat map is deceiving and makes certain places seem more distant from one another than they truly are. A flat map shows North America and Russia as farthest apart, but on a round globe, they are practically touching at Alaska. Likewise, if your geography of God is based on keeping a religious checklist and maintaining proper external behavior, hip-hoppers are about as far as one can get from God. The truth is, our real proximity to God isn't a matter of degrees based on what we do or don't do, but a matter of our depending on the reality of wholeness his presence provides.

Who knows how long I would have stumbled along with my own masquerade if Doug hadn't left his cell phone in that restaurant and a few parental-advisory-bearing CDs in his van. I guess God knew it would take some pretty unconventional means to wake me up. I just never thought Eminem would be the one helping me grow closer to God. I'm tired of eating crow on the journey, and I just don't have the time and energy to waste anymore on reveling in what's wrong with everyone else. Behind this nice person, I'm screwed up enough myself to go a long time without ever needing to make sport over other people's problems.

Actually, I plan to steal a few pages from those outrageous hip-hop types like Doug and others he introduced to me along the way. First, I'm going to stop caring about my image, reputation, and what people think. The game's over. No more smoke and mirrors. I believe there is a God and that he wants me to be whole. I'm going to be honest about the 50 Cent in me, and if all that gets messy for a while and my church friends can't handle it, that's okay. I'll just call Doug; he'll understand.

three

Waffle House Theology
(Wanda the Waitress)

Calling

SOME THINGS YOU LEARN KICKING AND SCREAMING ALL the way. I never knew "called" people worked as cooks, cashiers, or carpet installers and reckon it would have remained lost on me if it weren't for becoming one. The kicking and screaming began one frigid morning huddled in my car enjoying a few last puffs of heat while watching and waiting at Lot 93.

Like clockwork, the crew of Hispanics was already hard at it. One mixed mortar while another wheeled it across frozen mud, filled a large bucket, and hoisted it up with a makeshift pulley. Meanwhile, the sturdiest one of the group squatted down and in one fluid motion picked up six bricks pressed tightly together between both hands and heaved them blind high to another, who caught the stack, amazingly still pressed perfectly together. He set them down, replenishing the supply of his partner laying the brick with spade and mortar. This was a well-oiled bricklaying machine.

How did I get *here*? A master of divinity in hand and on my way to a doctorate. Staff member of the largest and most cutting-edge church in North America. Founder and pastor of a growing and innovative ministry. Executive director of an acclaimed inner-city nonprofit agency. Nationwide traveler, speaking out on international human rights tragedies. Now about to start yet another day of de-nailing lumber, hauling heavy sheets of plywood, tearing down wet, putrid drywall, and filling Dumpsters with construction debris strewn tornado-style all over the place. How . . . and why?

Glaring headlights prodded me back to reality. Danny was driving in with his battered '90s model S-10 pickup; he's the one bossing me around all day. I was already pondering my first handful of ibuprofen. Once esteemed for theological knowledge, wise counsel, speaking, and leadership, my value now was doing grunt work nobody else wants to do. No longer hobnobbing with movers and shakers of contemporary Christendom, my world now was rife with four-letter words and beer-drinking, chain-smoking, NASCAR-watching, deer-hunting Shania Twain fans. Feeling sick to my stomach, I hopped out into the bitter cold and pulled on my grungy work gloves for another day of meaninglessness. One more day of this and I might throw myself into a Dumpster.

Little did I know construction cleanup was just one stop on a long, winding road taking me seemingly farther and farther from "my calling." After divorce booted me from pastoral ministry, I began wandering around in a vocational wilderness, taking on executive leadership roles in the nonprofit world but never satisfied they were *it*. In order to find *it*, I decided to walk away from demanding positions to devote time and energy to searching. Thinking every person is born to *do* something: A-Rod, baseball; Bono, music; Gates, computers; Warren, purpose-driven guru; I was Jim Palmer, To Be Announced. In the meantime, my plan was to work odd jobs on the side until *it* emerged.

As time passed, the odd jobs got odder and the journey took unfamiliar and undesirable turns and paths. After the construction gig, I became a carpet salesman or, as the management insisted the position be called, "flooring specialist sales associate." In order to get that badge, I attended Carpet College in Dalton, Georgia, a one-week crash course on floor coverings including field trips to carpet manufacturing plants.

In case you're wondering, people have long transformed the ground on which they tread. Rugs and carpets have covered floors in virtually every part of the world since records began. Mechanized looms developed in 1841, Boston revolutionized carpet production. The three most widely available types of machine-made carpets are woven, tufted, and bonded. Research and use found carpet with a pile blend of 80 percent wool and 20 percent nylon offers the optimum balance of comfort, color retention, and wear. Whatever you do, remember, your selection is an expression of your individuality, although you must also consider the issues of warmth, sound, durability, traffic, maintenance, cleaning, and safety.

After receiving my carpet diploma, I considered adding the suffix PhC to my name: Jim Palmer, PhC. Surely it would impress someone too fainthearted to ask what PhC means.

The next stop was CJ's Café, a full-service cafeteria-style restaurant (meat and three, grill, salad bar, sandwiches, etc.) situated downtown inside a government building. I was hired to work the register, something I had never done—but how hard could it be? Well . . . ringing people up in lines on both sides, I was also responsible for making coffee, refilling silverware, and keeping the dessert tables full of fresh pies from the cooler. The cash register itself was a train wreck, with mismatched labels like the button reading "Chicken Club" now meaning the Meatball Sub. Receiving a busy signal when processing credit cards meant sprinting to the back office and yelling at Jeff the dishwasher to get off the phone with his girlfriend. I'd return to impatient stares and the surreal world of Ms. Ellie, who always accused me of giving her the wrong change, and Marvin, who couldn't fill out a check in less than five minutes if his life depended on it.

Clocking in daily at 5:30 a.m. required my rolling, and I mean rolling, out of bed at 4:30. I did morning prep (unloading the dishwasher, filling the hot chocolate/latte machine, cutting lemons, slicing bagels, arranging pastries, etc.) and ran the register during the breakfast stampede. We had thirty minutes to turn it around for lunch (cleaning tables, making iced tea, setting up the salad bar, filling Coke machines with ice, etc.), when the mayhem turned the picturesque salad bar into a war zone. At 2:00 p.m. we cleaned up the joint in a flurry of wiping, vacuuming, mopping, disassembling, stacking and wrapping. We then locked it up and crawled to our cars, hopefully beating the early rush hour. After a long week on my feet at the cafeteria, I realized how overrated sex is compared to the ecstasy of a foot massage.

My next tour of duty was Kohl's department store. The back half of the store, which included housewares (appliances, vacuum cleaners, luggage, etc.), domestics (towels, bedding, table linens, rugs, etc.), and seasonal (framed art, candles, seasonal items, etc.), became my world, or "sector" as they called it. Retail department store work simplified my theology in several ways. In seminary there was much debate over the nature of hell. After working the Christmas season, I am satisfied I could do a doctoral thesis on the "weeping and gnashing of teeth." I might spend twenty minutes properly folding and restacking bath towels, only to have some lady with too much time on her hands shake out two of every color, hold them up to the light!?!? . . . and toss them back in a pile without a thought. She would eventually end up over in seasonal, pulling out the picture frames and cramming the mess back on the shelf for me to organize . . . again. Given enough time, she would find her way over to domestics, where she would probably throw rugs in the aisles without picking them up.

Retail can get to you. Once, while in vacuum cleaners, I reasoned spending several years in prison would be worth silencing one man who wanted me to explain the pros and cons of every model. It's a freaking vacuum, for goodness' sake. How did I know? I went to carpet college, not vacuum cleaner academy! I was going crazy. I'd be on the ladder in the stockroom putting away merchandise and thinking to myself, *How many grill designs can George Foreman come up with?* I also wanted to give that Laura Ashley chick a piece of my mind! Once the architect of strategic plans for organizational growth and worldwide mission, I couldn't make heads or tails of the schematic giving proper shelf locations for each style of coordinating bath rugs and toilet seat covers. It could have been worse, which crossed my mind every time I walked past shoes; that section was anarchy.

With each sheet of plywood, carpet measurement, pot of coffee, and folded towel, I was sinking deeper and deeper into confusion and discouragement. I was barely able to pull my aching body out of bed for my construction job; how was I supposed to have my morning quiet time with God? My retail work schedule changed weekly but was mainly nights and weekends, leaving little time and energy for extracurricular (read church) activities. Once the pastor who chided people dozing off in services, I was now experiencing life on the other side. I was finding Christianity in the real world had all sorts of challenges I never experienced in my vocational ministry world.

I made a nice living in ministry-related positions with great insurance benefits. It was a rude awakening when my two hourly-pay jobs supplied half my previous salary without medical insurance. The day-to-day financial struggle was taxing, but the real struggle was the sense of failure I associated with my working in this "nonprofessional" world. It was humiliating when someone asked Pam, "So what's Jim doing now?" "Well, he's, ahhh, selling carpet." "Oh . . . really . . . that's nice." Working the restaurant register, people looked down on me like the scum of the earth, and retail shoppers treated me like a little servant boy. Didn't they know who I was? At Kohl's, my pride had me scurrying to hide among curtains or hurrying to the stockroom to avoid being seen by someone from my previous life. The day came when I was called up to run the register, and one came through my line. I died a slow death, carrying on painfully awkward conversation with someone who didn't know quite what to say to a spiritual guru now ringing up early-bird specials.

Perhaps any of these jobs would have been acceptable for a student working himself through college or as a part-time job to supplement family income, but not full-time employment for a grown man as *educated, gifted,* and *called* as I was. Well-intentioned Christian friends told me it was a shame and I should take a "step of faith" to get back into "ministry."

The first time I ever walked into a Waffle House was during this time of downward mobility. I often escaped to the one near the carpet store for a quick bite and perhaps a chapter or two of whatever book I was reading. Waffle House was my oasis; cheap, strong coffee and no chance of anyone I knew being there (they were all Cracker Barrel types). I don't ever remember knowing a "Wanda" before then. Living in Nashville by way of Gary, Indiana, Wanda was a talker who waited on me that first visit and practically every time I was in after that.

Though a petite and slender woman, Wanda had a sense of durability evident mostly in her strong forearms and hands. Her wiry auburn hair brushed her shoulders, and as a matter of course, she wore it tucked behind her ears and out of her dark brown eyes. Her fair face showed the wear of a difficult life, which included an abortion in her teens, alcoholism in her twenties, and an abusive marriage in her thirties, now struggling to piece it all back together pushing fifty.

I never met the manager, but for all practical purposes, Wanda ran the joint. Often balancing a large tray loaded with food on one hand while pouring coffee refills along the way with the other, she would continue her friendly, albeit opinionated banter with the guys sitting at the counter. She could declare you were full of it, which she often did to the regulars who enjoyed prying into her love life or the lack thereof, and you'd still want to give her a big hug. Calling me by name and genuinely interested in making conversation, she routinely patted me on the shoulder, making me feel she was glad I was there.

One afternoon after I took a table, Wanda appeared and noticed I was absorbed in one of my Christian books.

"Must be good, Jim?"

"Oh, hi, Wanda." Pointing to my book, "This? Yeah, it is good actually."

Squinting at the cover, "What is it?"

"Oh, it's just one of those spirituality books."

"Really. Honey, I read all that stuff. Started back in my AA days. Ever read those *Conversations with God* books by what's his name?"

"No, I've never read those. Are they good?"

"Oh, honey! Couldn't put 'em down. You gotta read 'em."

Suddenly, the two programmed proper evangelical questions for this sort of thing popped into my mind: *Do you know Jesus?* and *Do you attend church regularly?* I decided on the easier of the two. "Do you go to church anywhere, Wanda?"

"I work Sundays, hon."

A voice rings out "Order up!" and off she goes.

A while later she was back topping off my coffee and offering in an exacting tone, "Besides, I tried all that once and it never worked for me. I guess it does for some people. I could never be one of them." Pausing to fish creamers out of her apron, she said, "They don't want people like me. That's what I found out. Anyway, this is my church right here." Then she zipped away, giving me no opportunity to respond.

This was the first time I had ever seen Wanda visibly rattled. Feeling terrible, I said, when she returned with my check, "Wanda, look, I'm sorry if . . ."

"Jim, honey, now don't you go being sorry." She stole a corner of the seat across from me, put her hand on mine, and said, "Listen, hon, I just never seemed to fit in at church, you know? I'd sometimes be in my uniform, and folks stared like I was some kind of prostitute. I ain't no whore! I'm a waitress. Never finished high school, Jim. That preacher was way too smart for me. I ain't afraid to admit it. Let's just say all them fancy words don't mean much at Waffle House. Now, don't you think another thing about it, hon." Standing to gather up my plate and silverware, she offered these final words with a wink to console me: "Shoot, I might go back yet. Teach 'em a thing or two."

I don't know if Wanda ever went back to church, but she taught me a thing or two, some of which I could have gone without knowing. She talked about how over the years Christians were often her worst customers. They would come in all cheery and blessed after Sunday morning service, running her unmercifully with a table of eight and leaving loose change for a tip on a large bill. She remembered on one occasion coming upon a group to take their order and finding them in prayer. She respectfully waited until they were finished, but minutes later they complained their baked potatoes were too hard and iced teas too icy, which she gladly remedied. At the end of their meal they left only an evangelistic tract, which did little to pay Wanda's heating bill that month. For years, I prided myself on having right theology, but Wanda got me thinking about whether any theology can be "right" if it doesn't motivate you to treat people with love and respect. Let's just hope on Judgment Day that God doesn't leave it in the hands of waitresses, cashiers, and all the other invisible people in our world who are on the receiving end of what's truly in our hearts.

Out of the spotlight of "professional ministry," I was now fully immersed in a world of nobodies. I refused to accept this and reasoned with God that I had endured this trial long enough and needed to be back in "ministry." What sense did it make to be pining away somewhere folding towels, wasting my gifts, and abandoning my "calling"? When it became apparent God didn't share my way of thinking, I just flat-out got angry and enjoyed being miserable to show God just how horrendously he was treating me. I can be pretty dramatic and even tried the whole life-is-no-longer-worth-living-just-please-take-me-now thing.

Yet unnoticeably along the way, I was also getting to know, enjoy, and care about this cast of characters who were now part of my life. During breaks on the construction site, I talked sports with Michael, the drywall/painter guy, once a local high school sports megastar but not star enough to play college ball. To Michael, every general contractor was the enemy. He would continually threaten to walk off the job. I would calm him down, insisting he couldn't abandon me, because I hated painting. At CJ's, the other cashier, Candi, and I looked out for each other. We didn't mind picking up the slack if the other one was slammed or just having a crappy day. Sometimes she came to me for guy advice (couched in hypothetical scenarios) in her on-again, off-again, on-again, off-again relationship with her boyfriend, who first wanted to be a country singer, then a race-car driver, and then a real-estate tycoon like those midgets on TV, all the while working at Blockbuster.

Then there were Judy and John at Kohl's, married with grandchildren. Judy ran seasonal and domestics while John oversaw the cleaning crew. Well beyond retirement age, it killed me that they both still worked full-time trying to build their nest egg. Thankfully, as full-timers they had medical insurance when John had a stroke. He still managed to return to work a couple of months later. I would have long before quit Kohl's if it hadn't been for Judy, who practically worshipped me for being one of the few in her department who actually worked. I never told her, but in many ways she was the mom I'd always wished for. My soft spot for her still produces an excuse to go shopping there with hopes she's working so I can hug her.

These nobodies—Michael, Wanda, Candi, Judy, John, and many others—were now friends I cared about . . . and who cared about me. The notion began growing inside that perhaps I was "called"—to them. Maybe this way of living is "ministry," and God ordained these very connections and relationships. Side by side in the ebb and flow of daily living and working, God wanted to bless us through our knowing one another. Sure, it might not seem like much through the eyes of my graduating seminary class, but it sure mattered to them and to me. I felt I had discovered a missing link, experiencing meaningful relationship with God through others amid the wear and tear of real life. It all sounds nice in church on Sundays, but can you really know God and walk in his kingdom waiting tables, cleaning out dressing rooms, and framing houses? Maybe Jesus came as a poor common laborer to supply to all the ordinary of the world the resounding answer, "Yes, you can." The truth is, if it doesn't work there, it doesn't work anywhere.

God has been trying to free me from the burden of doing something spectacular for him. It has a way of distracting you from the opportunities to be salt and light right where you are. I'm starting to see that the "cup of cold water given in Jesus's name" sometimes means running the register by yourself during lunch so your heartbroken coworker can cry in the break room, or volunteering to reshelf all the returns in your area so a worn-out coworker twice your age won't have to. A kindness shown here, a listening ear offered there, a caring hug as you go might be the case for Christ a cynical waitress most needs. I'm starting to recognize that I am immersed in a sea of hurting people every day. If I simply pay attention and follow the promptings of the Spirit in all these little ways, my life is "ministry." One of my spiritual gifts is teaching, but I don't need to stand on a stage before a crowd to use it. God uses it in conversations with people like Wanda to help unravel the complex, far-off, unattainable version of Christianity she heard at church.

The other day I received a glossy brochure to attend a national pastors' conference in California. Opening it, I was suddenly staring into the eyes of an old buddy of mine I served with years ago on the staff of a megachurch in Chicago. Reading the caption under his picture, I learned he had become the pastor of a megachurch himself and was one of the main speakers for the conference. Feelings of sadness and regret fell over me. What had I accomplished with my life? What great thing had I done or would I ever do for God? All this time I had been searching and seemingly not finding *it*. Then the words of one of those divine nobodies entered my mind. Speaking as if he were God, he would say, "*I AM* what you are looking for." I'm starting to realize *it* begins and ends with knowing Jesus.

The next afternoon I went to the store to buy a new coffeemaker. I had busted the little spring contraption on the filter basket, making my old one worthless. Surprisingly, I found one on sale for only $9.99. (Of course, at home I could see why, when the plastic cup thermometer thingamajig popped off as I pulled it out of the box.) In the checkout line, things weren't going too well. The stressed-out woman working the register was waiting for someone in kidswear to check the price on a coat, which the customer was irately refuting. Meanwhile, the line grew longer and the people angrier. Giving the cashier drop-dead stares, people started mumbling hateful comments just loud enough for her to hear. "This is ridiculous." "Idiot." "How stupid." Finally, the miffed customer laid into the cashier with a piece of her mind and stormed off, leaving a mountain of merchandise for the gal to clear off.

After a manager came and cleared the register of the lost sale, the cashier continued ringing out customers. Her apologies were met by cold, hateful silence and bags snatched away in disgust. Finally, I was next in line. "Sir, I apologize for the wait today." Seeing her name tag, I replied, "No problem,

Nancy. You're fine. I'm in no hurry." As she stared at her screen, a lone tear slowly creeped down her face. Why? Was it because of the beating she had just taken? Maybe she was like me back at Lot 93, at the end of her rope. Taking my bag, I said something that surprised me since it was a little uncharacteristically bold for me. I looked her dead in the eye and said, "Nancy, I've been there, and it's going to be all right." She thanked me—not one of those quick, customary thankyous, but a deliberate, heartfelt one.

On my way to the car, Nancy's tear was still in my mind. I wondered if it was a tear of gratitude or hurt. Like me, Nancy was looking for Jesus. Maybe she experienced him in our brief encounter. I did. Knowing myself all too well, I know I was capable of being just as uncaring as the other customers. It was Christ living in and through me that enabled me to reach out to Nancy.

four

Death to the Phantom
(Worthless Grace)

Identity

IT GETS RIDICULOUSLY COLD IN ANGMAGSSALIK, GREENLAND, and Ivangorod, Estonia. I know. Set to my Internet home page, I routinely check the weather in these remote places along with the town where I grew up (Blacksburg, Virginia), our honeymoon location (Cape Cod), and where I dream of one day living (Santa Barbara, California). I discovered the fascinating far-off places of Greenland and Estonia at the public library not a mile from our front door. These days I am experiencing a personal learning renaissance. Perhaps this is God's way of balancing out the dark ages of my college years when education was sacrificed on the altar of campus evangelism and discipleship. (Okay, okay, maybe there were also one too many dorm Ping-Pong tournaments and weekend road trips.)

While some enroll in continuing education courses, I pick an aisle in the nonfiction section of our library and peruse subjects and titles until coming across something interesting. By using this method, I have acquired a range of knowledge that enables me to hold my own in conversation if any of the following subjects come up: the rise and fall of the Sumerians;

architectural nuances of an inviting street café; unique breed-
ing habits of the giant kangaroo rat (*Dipodomys ingens*); and
what really happened to Elvis. The library is way underrated
as a form of escape (remember Andy Dufresne in *The
Shawshank Redemption*?). I can spend ten bucks and roll the
dice on a movie or crack open a picture book of the Balearic
Islands at no cost and imagine soaking up the sun on a
rooftop patio overlooking the Mediterranean Sea. (Either
way, I have to sneak in my own supply of yogurt pretzels.)

Sometimes you see strange things in libraries. Once,
through a shelf of books, I spied a guy in the magazine section looking both ways before carefully slipping a *USA
Today* into his briefcase. Hey! I hadn't even read the sports
page yet. Then there's the time I saw the librarian at the
counter turn away from a departing (and apparently difficult)
customer and flip her the bird out of everyone's view except
mine at the water fountain. It made for a strange moment
when our eyes met, and it burst my bubble that all librarians
are mild-mannered Mother Teresa types whose greatest joy in
life is simply helping people find books.

One day while browsing, I came across a large picture
book of Ireland, each page a photograph of some aspect of a
day in the life of this legendary land accompanied by an
explanatory caption. Settling into my comfy chair, I set off to
the ancient island. Somewhere around Dublin the corner of
my eye caught something that hijacked my attention. All
decked out in a pretty pink dress with white lace was a sweet
little girl in a wheelchair. Her angel face was radiantly pale,
and her sandy-blonde hair was pulled back in a ponytail
sporting a big yellow bow. Frilly white stockings disappeared
into her sturdy white leather dress shoes, which were
strapped down tight to the folding metal rests beneath her

pigeon-toed feet. I could not turn away from this portrait of mangled beauty, despite knowing well enough that it isn't polite to stare at handicapped kids.

Kneeling down close beside the little girl is Dad. With one arm gently wrapped around her, he reads from an oversized storybook propped up in her lap. Slumped over against his shoulder, she is turned toward him, with the top of her precious head resting against the side of his face. She can't walk or sit up straight, and offers only an occasional groan. She's just sitting there unresponsive, seemingly oblivious, as Dad dutifully reads her a story, altering his voice to impersonate the different characters.

My mind began wandering, imagining this father's world. On bended knee is a man who must walk through life brokenhearted for his daughter, who will never sing silly songs, skate in the park, or dance at her prom. A dad who loves his little girl perhaps even more because of that but who will never hear "I love you, Daddy," whispered in his ear or receive a homemade Father's Day card with sunshine and stick people. She will never do most of the things a ponytailed little girl wants to do for her daddy. A tidal wave of sorrow crashed over me as I pictured my Jessica strapped in and slumped over in that wheelchair.

The lens of my soul zoomed in on her facial expression as she sits wrapped in her father's arms. Earnestly reading, she sits spellbound, gazing into his face with her mouth slightly open with a smile. He's glued to the book; she's glued to him. What does she see? What does she feel? She seems so content and peaceful, at home really, resting her head against Daddy's face, receiving his love. Then again, that's all she can do. She's not even capable of reciprocating her father's love, and yet I can see she is his most precious treasure. Perhaps most look upon this scene in pity. How terrible to not be able to function in the most essential ways; perhaps in the eyes of the world she is useless. Not to her father. To him she is priceless.

Taking all this in, a torrent of troubling thoughts rose from somewhere deep within me. Would God still love me if I couldn't do anything for him? What if I were useless and couldn't do even the basic things I had learned a good Christian does? What if I couldn't impact others in any significant way, lead someone to Christ, serve a person in need, teach others Scripture, be a leader? What if I couldn't even go to church or have a quiet time? What if I couldn't progress any further in my spiritual life? What if I were barely even capable of having an intelligent thought about God? What if . . .

Complicating the matter further, the handicapped girl with her doting dad festered the wound of my own father's rejection. Even before he left, he was never really there. To this day I cannot remember ever having a meaningful conversation with my father or a time when he looked me square in the eye and said he was proud of me or loved me. We never went on camping trips or to sporting events or worked on cars together. I tried out for the football team one year, hoping my father would take interest in me, but he never attended one of my games. Somewhere back there that curly-haired kid with gaps in his teeth and glasses held together by masking tape came to the unconscious but firm conclusion that he was badly defective, ugly, stupid, and worthless. This was the only logical explanation to a little boy for why his dad was so thoroughly indifferent toward him and eventually left home altogether.

I'll be honest, all that "inner child" stuff makes me a little squeamish, but I cannot deny that my childhood self-hatred has played out in my adulthood with this automatic and insatiable drive to prove to the world (mostly myself and God) that I am not the piece of dung something inside tells me I am. Despite my sound grasp of the doctrine of justification, for all practical purposes, if God is my "Father," then I am still the useless bumbling son needing to supply sufficient reason for God to like me. My born-again legal standing before God was sufficient for warding off his wrath, but the idea that God was proud and satisfied with who Jim Palmer was seemed like a pipe dream. Following me into the library that day was this phantom Christian I had created through years of being the kind of saintly person with whom I surmised God would be pleased. The whole drill seemed to be to strive hard to fulfill God's expectations and play your 1 John 1:9 card when you failed, earning you the right to start over and try harder.

Sitting there, a heavy weariness set in and I wanted to cry. I'm so tired of trying to get God to like me. I'm terrified of being abandoned and left alone in life. It had already happened a few times with people it's not supposed to. Having tasted of God's love, I didn't want to lose it. Making things work with God was my last great hope in life, and I couldn't afford to mess it up. If I drove God away, who was left? I knew when I died I would go to heaven, but something deep within needed and longed for God now. I worked hard to stay on my game (daily quiet times, attending church, leading groups, and teaching classes) as I envisioned God in heaven perpetually asking, "What have you done for me lately?" I was desperate and willing to take whatever rest I could get, even if it was just an hour in a comfortable chair eating yogurt-covered pretzels and escaping to Ireland in photographs.

But then there was this out-of-order child in the wheelchair . . . useless yet priceless. She can't even sit up straight, but someone has gone through all the trouble of doing her up in bows and frills. An occasional grunt is Dad's only reward for giving his all in reading her the story. There's nothing she can really do *for* him, but she doesn't need to do anything; her father simply loves her. She's just slumped over, gazing into his face, receiving his love.

I've never spoken in tongues, healed anyone, or reached the blissful state of nirvana, and I probably wouldn't even know the yin from the yang if I ran right into it, but sitting in the public library thumbing through photographs of Irish foxhounds, farmers, and pubs, a picture of a girl and her father came down from heaven. Somehow, right before my very eyes, the Spirit transformed this sight into a snapshot of God and me, offering a completely new set of "What if . . ." questions.

What if I'm the girl slumped over in the wheelchair? What if there isn't anything I can do "for" God? What if he just wants me to lean against his face and receive his love? What if this phantom Christian I've been chasing is just a big distraction from resting in what God wants to freely give? What if my value and worth to God are not contingent on what I *do*? Maybe this is why I'm so tired inside. My soul has only so much energy, and the bulk of mine is being drained through striving to earn God's love and acceptance. What would it be like to truly know there isn't one more thing I ever have to do for God in order for him to be pleased with me?

I am so afraid. I'm holding on to all these things I feel I must do to stay on God's radar. Who will I be if I have nothing left to hold on to? Who will I be when I stand before God with empty hands? Maybe this is what God is trying to tell me. He wants me to open my clenched fists and discover I am not what I do but what he wants to give me. And what he wants to give me is love and life, unconditional love and life. God placed the little girl right before me and gave me the eyes to see the deeper meaning of her handicapped condition. Until I understand I literally cannot *do* anything *for* God to achieve worth and value in his eyes, I won't stop trying. Maybe God wants me to stop trying.

Jesus once said, "Apart from me you can do nothing." Wasn't Jesus essentially saying there is nothing *we* can do of value for God on our own? Think about it—isn't it a little silly to think there is anything God *needs* me to do *for* him? He's *God*! However, God did create me for the purpose of knowing him and has placed his life inside me so I can know him. God wants me to experience him as life, peace, freedom, wholeness, and joy; and as I trust and depend upon his presence within, I come to know him in these ways, and God is pleased. If you're building a sandcastle on the beach a few feet from the ocean, what sense does it make to be hauling Dixie cups of water one by one from your hotel room across the street on the fifteenth floor? There's an endless supply right before you for packing sand and filling moats. Maybe "accepting Christ" isn't so much a one-time thing we do as a formula for escaping hell in the afterlife, but rather a lifelong process of learning to depend on the sufficiency of Christ within for what we most deeply need and desire. His life fills our empty moats of worth, purpose, and love.

Though I had a seminary degree and could wax eloquent from the Pauline Epistles about "unmerited favor," somehow God could see I needed a little help to truly understand. He arranged for that angel in a wheelchair to be right in place, knowing I needed to witness a dad loving his daughter who couldn't do anything for him and didn't need to. Watching her peacefully and contentedly resting against Daddy's face, I could see she had found what my soul was yearning for. I needed to know a heavenly Father's love that did not require my striving to maintain it. Maybe you can't get the "know he is God" part right until you get the "be still" part down.

The other day Jessie and I were enjoying a pleasurable summer afternoon at the town park. While swinging her, I spotted a mom pushing a quadriplegic young boy down the sidewalk. Jessica saw too. She watched intently, and the question eventually came, "Daddy, what's wrong with that boy?" After a lengthy explanation, trying to explain in six-year-old terms, Jessica became unusually quiet and continued watching. Without warning she finally responded, "Well, he's still a boy." A smile filled my face as I replied, "Yes, sweetheart, he's still a boy." There are some things you just are no matter what.

I never actually met the handicapped girl or her father in the Ireland picture book, but I learned two further things by reading about them. The little girl has cerebral palsy, and her name is Grace.

five

What the Sheep Do We Know!? (The Kids of Silent Rocks Farm)

Openness

> "Don't be afraid," the prophet answered. "Those who are
> with us are more than those who are with them."
> And Elisha prayed, "O LORD, open his eyes so he may see."
> Then the LORD opened the servant's eyes, and he looked
> and saw the hills full of horses and chariots of fire all
> around Elisha.
>
> —2 Kings 6:16–17 NIV

I WONDER IF THERE'S MORE TO THIS EXISTENCE THAN logic, science, or the five senses can explain.

We have explored galaxies and conquered cyberspace, but what if there is a larger fabric of reality beyond the immediately recognizable or explainable? Look around and within you right now. What if you're seeing and experiencing only the tip of the iceberg? Could another dimension of life and living exist? Notice where there appears to be nothing. Are you sure that's all there is before you? Could this space actually teem with possibilities more real than the chair you are sitting in? Reach your hand high into the air and imagine unzipping the supposed reality around you. With both hands, slowly pull the unzipped halves apart and peer inside, and wonder. Do you see it? "See what?" you say. Maybe there's nothing . . . or maybe there is and you just don't perceive it. (*Note to reader: I've not been toking wacky tobaccy.) What percentage of knowledge about all reality—physical, spiritual, divine, human, etc.—do you figure you possess? How about all of humankind combined? Do you know 5 percent, 3 percent, .00001 percent? Have you ever wondered what exists in that other percentage we don't know?

Somewhere in my passage from childhood through adolescence to adulthood, I stopped wondering. My religion and education removed mystery from life, supplying the essential questions and all the right answers. What was left to wonder about? Then one day, in the humdrum of everyday life—working, churching, consuming, escaping, parenting, surviving—I stumbled over something. Actually, it wasn't a some*thing* but a some*one*, a bunch of someones. Studying the Scriptures in the original biblical languages of Hebrew and Greek in seminary, it took a group of tiny tots to show me what it actually means in plain English. Let's just say I'm starting to believe there really is a zipper with something staggeringly expansive behind it.

Pam and I sometimes have difficulty remembering what life was like before our daughter, Jessica. Our study used to be a quaint and quiet refuge wrapped in books. Though we live in a small house, it still felt like getting away when slipping in with our coffee (Jim) and tea (Pam) to indulge in fine literature (Pam) or engage in profound theological scholarship (Jim). Okay, so I occasionally glanced at the sports page. Okay, okay, I read every stinking word of it. After Jessica, the room gradually succumbed to becoming a sprawling Little People city, filled with American Girl gear and a life-size play kitchen with tons of plastic food, one-third of which is lost in the abyss of our front room couch. Scandalously or, if you like, somewhat appropriately, my master of divinity diploma and distinguished theological treatises now share shelf space with books such as *If You Give a Mouse a Cookie.*

I grew up Catholic, became a Baptist, attended an Evangelical Free Church seminary, and pastored a nondenominational church. Through the twists and turns, the common denominator of all those years in church was my dependency upon services, clergy, and programs to dispense God and facilitate my Christianity. My spirituality was largely doing church, but deep inside I hungered for something more. Ultimately, I decided to break from organized Christianity to see if God was real and could be known beyond the structures of institutional church. Well, I should say *we* decided—Pam, Jessica, and me. We and a few other families we had met along the way began testing the waters on what it might mean to orient our day-to-day lives around knowing God, one another, and the other people God had placed around us. We hadn't fully thought through what it all was going to look like. For example, unplugging from organized church meant doing without a children's minister or a Christian education program to nurture Jessica. We were now solely responsible for guiding our daughter through spiritual waters.

When visiting Kit in Connecticut, I noticed him more than once purposefully calling over his kids to discuss their thoughts on God. It was odd that Kit seemed to be doing this not for their benefit but his, as if they knew something he didn't. Asking about it, he spouted off something about how children move with ease in the "world of the transcendent," whatever that meant. (Sounded a bit too New-Agey for me.) Remembering this and giving Kit the benefit of the doubt, I contacted him, seeking input to the discussions Pam and I were having about encouraging Jessica in her own relationship with God.

Kit put me in contact with a friend of his named Betty, who described this thing called an "atrium" where little children gathered to explore and experience God together. The idea already sounded a little flaky, and alarm bells went off when I discovered this little kiddy utopia used no teacher or curriculum. Okay, who kept these children from killing one another, and who taught them the Bible? I had enough VBS experience to know unsupervised kids left to themselves are little time bombs waiting to explode. I'm no James Dobson, but what about those strong-willed kids (aren't all of them strong-willed?) needing structure and discipline? At least back when I picked up Jessica from Sunday school, I was given a bunch of papers that proved she had actually learned something worthwhile in class.

Betty sensed my skepticism and took the time to explain her involvement in something she called the Catechesis of the Good Shepherd, a Montessori-based children's program developed by a Catholic woman in Rome named Sofia Cavalletti. Since I didn't have a Vatican dictionary to decode it all ("atrium," "Catechesis," "Montessori"?), she tried translating her explanation into Baptist terms.

According to Betty, research and personal experience show that children have a mysterious but undeniable attraction to God. Multitudes of well-documented cases exist where children have told of encounters with God in the very first years of life and know things about God no one had previously told them. She used a "Kit term" in describing children as "quintessential metaphysical beings" (these people have seen one too many episodes of Star Trek) who possess untrained capacities for experiencing ultimate immaterial reality. Betty explained that all children are naturally proficient in giving and receiving love and are connected to a source of joy flowing deep within them, making them especially able to know God, who, according to Betty, is the essence of both love and joy.

She also spoke of an intuitive knowledge unique to children for knowing truth beyond the capacities of mere rational knowledge, which enables them to experience the mystery and beauty of the kingdom of God as a real and present reality. Betty further detailed how children are especially able to comprehend and internalize spiritual truth through the language of metaphor and story, Jesus's most preferred modes of communication.

The Catechesis of the Good Shepherd takes seriously these spiritual characteristics of children and provides an environment that respects and nurtures these capacities. The name is based on Jesus's use of the shepherd metaphor to describe his loving and caring relationship with his children, his sheep.

Betty sought to calm my anxiety about my daughter's spiritual growth by assuring me that God desired relationship with Jessica, and the Spirit would faithfully cultivate this reality in her life. This took quite a while to compute (and still does . . . picture my mind as one of those room-sized IBM computers back in the late '70s operating at half a gigahertz), since I didn't seem to have this confidence in the Spirit even for myself. Life beyond institutional forms of church feels freeing at first, but then you start wondering how you are going to grow without all the sermons and classes. Jesus said about the Spirit in the Gospel of John, "He will take you by the hand and guide you into all the truth there is" (John 16:12 MSG). Maybe the gift of the Spirit is God's primary provision for a spiritual life and that is why Jesus emphasized it.

The very words Betty used to describe the spirituality of children were foreign to me. Mystery? I thought Christianity was about morality. Joy, beauty, and love? What about obedience, sacrifice, and commitment? Betty said the kingdom of God is the magnet of irresistible force God uses in attracting both young and old. I thought the point was Jesus's punching my ticket to heaven in the afterlife, but these kids, Betty said, knew better. Unseen by human eyes (or was it adult eyes?), the kingdom of God had already come and was delightfully real to them now. Yikes, where had I been? How'd I miss it?

Betty encouraged me to go check out a group of children gathering weekly for the Catechesis of the Good Shepherd at a church in downtown Nashville. Upon arriving I began exploring the enchanting room with child-sized tables, chairs, and shelves filled with wooden figures and backgrounds, and a variety of other things to feel, shake, mix, smell, taste, or move around. Quietly and calmly, a group of about fifteen three- to six-year-olds peacefully but joyfully entered the room. I didn't know what to make of this. Maybe that Cavalletti woman had drugged them. Did I need to call *60 Minutes*? Eagerly dispersing, the kids went to the shelves and carefully began removing things and placing them on the floor and tables. The space came alive.

One little girl poured flour into two bowls, to one adding a dash of yeast. She added water to each and began mixing. *Hmmm, you can't tell which one has the yeast.* Returning later, it was obvious. The one with yeast had mysteriously transformed itself from a little mound of flour into a large lump of dough. Across the room, a couple of young boys were inspecting tiny seeds in the palms of their hands. As with the yeast, Jesus says the kingdom of God is like these tiny living organisms. Comparing them to a photograph of a tall mustard tree, the boys were struck by the obvious. It begins so small but becomes large.

Over in the corner, children joined an adult on the floor sitting cross-legged behind a gated pasture made of wood and painted green with three-dimensional figures of a shepherd and ten sheep. Before captivated eyes, she slowly read from the Gospel of John about Christ the Good Shepherd while she slowly and deliberately moved each figure according to the story. The shepherd figure went out of the sheepfold and called each of the ten sheep by name. The gate was opened, and one by one each of the ten sheep was carefully walked out of the sheepfold close to the Shepherd in response to his loving and familiar voice. The children were so filled with joy.

In the center of the room, two girls were reenacting Jesus's parable comparing the kingdom of God to a merchant looking for fine pearls. A wooden merchant's shop sat on a mat with a basketful of fine jewels inside. Hidden behind the shelves was a small shell containing a priceless pearl. Little hands moved around the wooden merchant figure, who eventually and suddenly came across this precious pearl. Through the girl's facial expression and verbal response, the merchant was dumbfounded and overjoyed. "It's so beautiful!" The merchant rushed back to his shop in excitement and gladly sold all his jewels to buy the pearl. The girls found plenty to wonder about. The pearl didn't visibly look any different from the merchant's other small fine jewels, but it was. *Hmmm, what is the pearl? Is it God's love?* "We are the pearls," one said.

One of the families we were getting to know, the Williamses, lived on forty acres located about an hour outside the city, which they named Silent Rocks Farm. They were the homesteading and homeschooling types who raised goats and chickens. Being Mr. City Slicker, I never figured I'd find myself hanging out with people who read books titled *Raising Meat Goats for Profit* (my apologies to my vegetarian friends). It also took a while for me to trust that I wouldn't die from drinking goat milk or eating farm-fresh eggs (you know, before they add all those chemicals to make them safe).

After experiencing the Good Shepherd myself, I decided to send an e-mail, hoping to find someone locally who might have heard of it. I included the Williamses, figuring people who grow their own wheat and make their own soap might have come across something so off the beaten path as this. Since the Catechesis of the Good Shepherd was developed by Catholics, there probably aren't ten Baptists in all the country who have even heard of it. Joanna Williams was one of them. I first met Joanna while attending the same Baptist church, but now discovered she had been involved in a Good Shepherd atrium while living in Atlanta.

A couple more families joined our group, and we decided to start our own atrium. In addition to what Joanna had stored away in boxes, we began making our own materials, cutting, sanding, painting, sculpting, gluing, and laminating. Each week, on the Williamses' spacious, peaceful farm, Joanna facilitates the atrium with a helper while the remaining adults hang out, drink coffee, and enjoy front-porch conversation while overlooking farmland as far as the eye can see. From time to time each of us sits in to observe and be part of the experience with our children. Sometimes the children bring their parents special creations they have made. A special log is kept, recording the spontaneous things they do and say as they encounter God and explore spiritual realities.

One Sunday on the farm, a provocative thought entered my

mind while watching Joanna give a Good Shepherd presentation with the wooden shepherd and sheep. Maybe our children are trying to tell us something. Remembering back to our organized church days, whenever I sat Jessica down to flesh out moral lessons from an Old Testament story or review memory verses about obeying God, she seemed uninterested, which concerned me. But in the atrium, she and the other children were filled with joy by the notion of the Good Shepherd and his sheep. Pulling the materials onto the floor, they became the little flock familiar with the Shepherd's voice and joyfully following right behind him. Come to think of it, Jessica is fascinated by the picture in our home showing Jesus as an actual shepherd surrounded by sheep and carrying one in his arms. Something about that image deeply connects her with God.

A child's little revelations and epiphanies are easily passed over by adults' eyes and ears. When presented with Jesus's parable comparing the kingdom of God to a man searching for fine pearls, the children saw the kingdom of God as "beautiful," as something "you love." I look at that same passage, and all I can see is how he had to sell everything to purchase them. Maybe they are right and Jesus wants us to see the beauty of God's kingdom and the love it inspires. I'm inclined to say, "That's neat," and still move hastily to the calculation of what it's going to cost me. Could belonging to the kingdom of God be more than endless rules and dutiful sacrifice? With Christ hidden within us, maybe he's doing the mysterious work of yeast and mustard seeds, radically converting us into new, free, whole people.

Amazingly, these children aren't scared or hindered by mystery; rather, they pursue it, opening themselves to ever-widening spiritual horizons. I wonder if Jesus taught in parables because he knew divine realities are too large to be fully grasped by the human mind. Being mysteries in the classic sense of the word, perhaps they can only be hinted at through symbols and metaphors. I am also struck by the simplicity in which the children receive and celebrate the ways of God's kingdom. Jesus said, "Don't worry." The kids respond with, "Oh, I see. With Jesus, I don't have to worry anymore; he'll take care of me. Okay, great! I won't worry anymore;" I say to myself, "They don't, like, actually believe that . . . do they?" Sure, I guess technically Jesus did say, "Don't worry," but . . ." I can see why Jesus directs us to children as models of faith who unveil something about God and his kingdom. Despite my Christology classes in seminary, maybe Jesus most wants me to know him as does the little girl who picked up a miniature wooden sheep and set it atop the wooden shepherd's shoulder, seeming lost in time with closed eyes and a smile beaming across her face.

There are enough mixed metaphors in Jesus's parables to drive a high school lit teacher crazy, but it all made perfect sense to these little ones. Okay, there's this kingdom of God. Well, sort of. It's not like a *kingdom* kingdom; you know, like a place you visit with castles. It's more like a tiny seed inside you that mysteriously grows into a huge tree. Or a pinch of yeast mixed in a mound of flour, if you prefer. A king? Of course there is a king . . . kind of. Well, he's actually a shepherd, and the citizens are, well, sheep, of course; that is, if they're not the pearls, you know, then the king would be a merchant shepherd king. Make sense? If they can get it, why can't I? My problem is I just don't believe it because I want to overanalyze it and complicate it. We started this whole thing out of concern for the spiritual formation of our children, but now I'm wondering if God wasn't mostly trying to get us to realize we must become like children to understand.

I recently saw a movie called *What the Bleep Do We*

Know!? With quantum physicists as guides, the film delves into the provocative mystery of the nature and structure of reality and the accompanying spiritual implications. A companion sixty-page study guide offered on the Internet explores subjects such as the "psychospiritual consciousness revolution" and parapsychology (telepathy, clairvoyance, precognition, psychokinesis). It all seemed pretty wacky to me, but I learned there's a growing cultlike attraction to the movie, perhaps because of the increasing number of people seeking more expansive spiritual realities beyond what they've found in traditional religion. In all those hours spent painting sheep, shepherds, merchants, and angels, I had plenty of time to ponder my own spirituality as a Christian. Sadly, I realized it was actually pretty *un*spiritual—moral, intellectual, behavioral, emotional, but not really "spiritual."

Jesus taught about the kingdom of God more than any other subject and once said, "The kingdom of God is within you" (Luke 17:21 NIV). He also spoke of the truth that "will set you free" (John 8:32 NIV), and Paul referred to a dimension where "I no longer live, but Christ lives in me" (Galatians 2:20 NIV). These are but a few sayings of Jesus that lead me to believe there is a zipper. There's a whole other world, a kingdom, if you will. There are no empty spaces. The catch is, Jesus said, you have to be like a child to get it. I have to start believing he never would have said this if he hadn't planned on making this real within me. My religion provides way too small a wineskin to contain all that Jesus wants to give.

Based on my experience with the kids up at Silent Rocks Farm, I have my own movie idea. Try this on. It's titled *The Matrix Re-Reloaded* (pretty original, huh?). In the opening scene, two humanoids dressed in black step out of some otherworldly dimension into little Sally's room. Snatched from bed, she is transported to the Institute of Noetic Sciences hidden at the center of the universe where sinister minds seek to seize global consciousness in order to rule the cosmos. Seated all alone at a table in a small room, Zeo appears in wave particles and sits down across from her. Addressing her in a calm but intense tone, he says, "My dear, sweet Sally, tell us what you know." Feeling around in her dress pocket, she pulls out a little wooden sheep and sets it in the center of the table. Utterly befuddled, Zeo's expression demands an explanation. As Sally slowly leans forward and prepares to speak, Zeo moves close expectantly. Sally reaches for Zeo's hand, opens it, and places the sheep in it and whispers, "There's more than you think."

Last night before going to bed, we all went into Jessica's room. After reading a portion of Scripture together, Pam lit a candle, placed it on a chair, and turned off all the lights. We decided we were going to sit together in the silence and listen to God for anything he might want to say to us. We sometimes do this as a family. After sitting silently for a good while, we went around and told what, if anything, God said. With a sweet smile, Jessica shared what God spoke to her. Right now I am looking at the misspelled words she scribbled down in her little journal. This is what God said to her: "Jessie, you are my child and I love you." She believes him.

six

The Black Hole of Intimacy (Laddie the Dog)

Depression

Warning: *If you are on meds for depression, you might want to get them handy. If you aren't on meds for depression, I certainly hope you don't have to go on them as a result of reading this chapter.*

SOME DAYS I AWAKE WITH A HEAVY DESPAIR AND ICY deadness at the pit of my soul. I sometimes lay my hand across my chest searching for a heartbeat, just to be sure. The thought of taking a shower exhausts me. There's no rhyme or reason for when it strikes. Pulling myself out of bed, I begin trudging robotically through the day with total detachment. Only the sense of responsibility for my family and the habit of living for forty years keep me alive.

Many times I have been in this condition at church when someone asked how I was doing, and I replied, "Fine." I've responded like this so many times, one day I decided to look it up. To be "fine" is to be "optimally functioning with freedom from disease or abnormality." So my answer is a bald-faced lie. But after all, lying seems to be consistent with church rules of engagement—pleasant questions, pleasant answers, even if they are untrue. What am I supposed to say? "Hi, Jim, how are you?" "Funny you asked. Well, I'm at this place where I just don't think I can go on with my life anymore. It all seems so pointless, including your asking me that question, because I know you don't really want to spend the time to really listen to me describe my despair, nor do you really care to know about it. I'm not faulting you, because I don't even care that you don't care. I pretty much don't care about anything right now. I'm just trying to say that I feel utterly desolate inside and caught in the clutches of some unrelenting darkness that won't let me go. Not to worry: in a short while I'll be in bed and this hell will be over for a few short hours, but anyhow, there's always tomorrow . . . So, how are you?"

I remember as a young boy being awakened by the sound of church bells that rang out from the valley, rolling across town with a melody I can still hum in my head. The bells set my mind at ease and stirred an ember of hope that perhaps this new day would be better than the one before. But like the composition of the bells, the days of my youth endured unchanged. The ringing of hope gave way to fret-filled nausea as dissonant vibrations cautioned the commencement of yet another day. Years later, upon returning home one spring, I drove down the long, winding valley road early one morning to learn why the bells no longer rang. Surrounded by grazing hills and farmland, the once unblemished white clapboard church stood partially collapsed, bearing old scorch marks of a ruinous blaze. Windows down with the motor running, I sat for a while haunted by recollections of my abused childhood. I wished to bury my past there beneath the weeds and rubble, but those memories rode back with me up that forsaken valley road.

I grew up in a small town in southwestern Virginia nestled

on a plateau in the New River Valley with the Blue Ridge Mountains towering on one side and the Alleghenies on the other. As the summer sun's blazing brilliance faded slowly behind the gently sloping peaks, deep, aching loneliness simmered in my soul. Looking back, I am amazed I ever escaped those mountains alive, as the valley still reminds me of my painful past. The awareness of being alone was real to me at a very young age. My mother's chronic depression and alcoholism, the abandonment of my father, and my older brother's brutality and addictions so dominated everyday life, I was left to grow up in the obscure shadows of what professionals refer to as a highly destructive dysfunctional family. Oddly, I remember very little from the days of my early childhood, and yet there is one memory that has endured these many years. I suppose the memory has found a permanent place in me because it has taken me back a thousand times to my life as a young boy. It's the memory of being alone and afraid in my room with the door locked. Well, not completely alone. There was Laddie.

Laddie was my brother's dog. This collie and I had one unfortunate thing in common. In the maddening chaos, all the people who were supposed to be taking care of us forgot we existed. For Laddie this meant days, months, and years of being tied with a short chain to a stake in the backyard or crammed into a little crate in our garage. For a long time I was afraid of him because he seemed mean and aggressive. Then it dawned on me he was this way because he rarely got food or clean water, was hardly ever bathed or groomed, and lived in solitary confinement except when my brother chased him around the yard and beat him for pulling up the stake. Though it went mostly unnoticed, I quietly decided to adopt Laddie as my dog. In addition to feeding and bathing him regularly, I allowed him to hang out with me in my room even though he wasn't supposed to be in the house. Somewhere along the way in all those hours together behind that locked door, Laddie and I arrived at a certain understanding; we needed each other if we were going to make it.

I would sometimes sink into the black hole of anguish and loneliness in the corner of my room. Inevitably Laddie would shuffle over and stretch out lengthwise on the floor facing me. With his head down between those big paws, he would look straight up at me. Making eye contact would prompt a slow tail wag, but he remained dutifully quiet and still until welcomed into my lap. I talked and he listened. I cried; he lay there next to me. Often we dozed off together back-to-back on my bedroom floor. Maybe he needed attention; maybe I needed a presence until the darkness passed. All I know is that neither of us was quite right from all we had endured, but we both seemed to accept this about each other, and somehow that mattered.

A lot of years have separated then from now. I'm finding it takes time, maybe even a lifetime, to grieve your real losses and possess them as your own. Though I'm all grown up on the outside, I've not come along quite so quickly on the inside. I have not easily let go of the secret hope that somehow it could all magically be erased or made right or the wishful expectation that someone or something could compensate for the sadness. For me, "discipleship" has been getting to that place where I dared to say, "This is my life, the life that is given to me, and it is the life I have to live. It is unique, and nobody else will ever live it. I have my own history, and a wounded childhood is part of it. No one else will carry the same sorrow or face the same darkness. I have my own life to live, and I will live it the best I can."

I made the mistake for so many years of running away

from my past. I eventually decided to walk into the darkness rather than try to outrun it, to let my sadness take me on a journey wherever it would lead, and allow it to transform me rather than to think I could somehow avoid it. Sometimes I turn around and surprisingly discover little ways God is healing wounds and making me whole, but I'm still not "fine."

To be honest, in many instances the version of Christianity I had fashioned and the church people I associated with didn't help. Beneath the weight of "becoming like Christ" I thought myself a complete failure; Jesus didn't walk around depressed or have days when he couldn't get out of bed. I would hold my Bible high in church, repeating the words "I am what it says I am; I have what it says I have," and drive home depressed. What seemed to be working beautifully for everyone else, obviously, I wasn't getting. What was wrong with me? Good, mature, Spirit-filled, close-to-God Christians are not depressed. The prescription was to try harder.

Though I tried leaving my depression at the door, I failed miserably; and subsequently, once inside, I felt ashamed. *You're not supposed to be depressed if you are a Christian.* After all, it's "non-Christians" who are the miserable ones needing to see our ecstatic, smiling, problem-free faces and hear our radical transformation stories if they are ever to find Jesus. You're never going to grow a church with a bunch of despondent people moping around!

I remember once being in a small group where the leader asked people to share a current struggle. After folks shared things like missing quiet times, sick family members, and job annoyances, in a moment of ill-advised transparency I spoke of my depression. The idea of a depressed Christian scandalized the group, and the leader later called me with a Bible verse to memorize that he said would make me feel better.

Practically every time I saw him, rather than asking me directly about my depression, he asked how I was coming along in memorizing the Scripture. It seemed to me that the church rules on depression were avoidance or denial. Things people said, such as, "It's a beautiful day. Why don't you go out and soak up some sunshine"; "But you're such a wonderful person, Jim. Look at all the good you've done"; and "I know exactly how you feel" made matters worse.

Come to think of it, if my church friends had simply done what Laddie did, they would have made a difference. What a blessing to have had someone present to my pain without trying to fix it, to simply stand respectfully at the edge of the mystery and misery of my depression. To this day when I am caught in the throes of depression, what most brings relief is a simple foot rub from Pam. In some strange way, this often seems to bring relief and release. I'm starting to see how the spiritual, physical, mental, and emotional parts of me are interdependent. Massage therapy sounds like a strange area of service and ministry within the church, but I'll throw out the thought that it might be one of the most important ways of loving and ministering to people who struggle with depression.

There was the day as a young boy when I was told my father had left for good. We had to sell our house and move into a small apartment on the other side of town across from an old graveyard. My heart dropped to the pit of my stomach when my mother informed me Laddie wasn't going with us. An ad was placed in the town newspaper, and soon the day came when we coaxed him with a doggie treat into the back of our brown station wagon to take him to his new owners. My older sister drove, and I sat quietly in the passenger seat, looking out the window. A little ways down the road she asked if I was okay. I couldn't speak, fighting with every ounce of energy I could muster to levy the flood of emotions coursing through my soul. Still, a silent river of tears began to flow even as my outward gaze hid the enormity of my suffering.

We sat in silence all the way there and all the way back. I could not even get out of the car when Laddie was handed over to his new owners. I've never been close to anyone in my family, but I often imagine I could be close to my sister. We made this mysterious, unspoken connection driving away from that house, because she knew we had left behind the biggest piece of me, gone forever.

I figure everyone has a car ride or two they won't ever forget. I remember my first real car date in high school, going to pick up Lori Smith and managing to slide into a big ditch on the side of the road right in front of her house. Saved forever in my mind is the look on her father's face in my rearview mirror as I spun mud all over his face as he tried to push me out. Then there was that time when my college buddies and I piled into a van in Tennessee heading north to a conference in Illinois, rotating drivers while others slept, never noticing our wrong turn until crossing the Ohio state line. But most of all, there's an aching sadness that wells up from deep within me every time I play back that station-wagon drive with Laddie. I guess there are just some hurts that always travel with you.

I escaped childhood with two photographs of Laddie. As the years passed from college dorm to apartment to house, I lost track of the pictures and figured they had been lost or misplaced along the way. One day, while hunting for light-bulbs in our bedroom closet, I came across a small box hiding on the top shelf. Inside was a stack of old pictures, and I began flipping through them. When a photograph of Laddie appeared, I smiled but hurt inside. I loved that dog, and even now there's some part of a little boy still inside who misses him. Studying the picture of that long-muzzled old friend, it hit me that Laddie's companionship sustained me through some of the most horrendous experiences of my childhood. I know it must sound silly, but the attentive and caring presence of that dog often rescued me.

The particular photograph showed Laddie stretched out across the floor in my childhood room where he normally positioned himself as I unraveled into a muddle of fear and despair. I still remember taking the photo on the morning of that fateful day we sent Laddie away. Looking at the picture, memories filled my mind of that aching boy hunched over in the corner of his room. As I lingered in sadness, gazing at that picture, another image began to fill my mind. I started to see the photograph differently. Now there was a man sitting on the floor next to Laddie, as if he were offering his own caring presence. It was strangely clear to me that this was Jesus. Strange because, over the years, I had been conflicted inside over how God was connected to my childhood, and I often wondered where God was during those horrific times.

The image of Jesus sitting next to Laddie staggered me. The implications were overwhelming. Jesus was always there. Through all those years when it seemed God was absent, he was actually present—seeing, listening, caring, and hurting with me and over me. Perhaps my feelings and five senses are not always a reliable guide to the facts of God. God can be intimately present even if it feels like he's nowhere to be found. Whenever I sank down into my black hole of depression, I often felt unbearably alone and abandoned by God, but now I was seeing this wasn't true. Maybe that's what the psalmist meant as he pondered the unbroken presence of an attentive and loving God, and wrote, "Even the darkness will not be dark to you" (Psalm 139:12 NIV).

Sitting in the closet, I realized both the little boy then and the grown man now were not alone, and I felt peace. For years, my depression was like being shut inside a tiny house with windows tightly shut, shades pulled down, and door locked. Despite being surrounded by the warmth of the sun, I had no awareness of it. In the darkness, I sat longing for light, pleading for light, wondering what I had done that the light had been taken away from me. But now I see I was and am actually surrounded by light. God longs for my awareness that his divine love holds me, and that awareness brings healing and a sense of wholeness. God's love is there in the darkness of depression with me, there next to me in my little locked house, sharing my pain, holding me closely, and offering the light of his love.

I used to be ashamed of my depression, but now I see it's a secret trapdoor to God. When it hits, I sink down into that black hole and often find Jesus there. I acquired in seminary a lot of theologically correct answers to the question of who Jesus is. Virtually every religious holiday stirs up debate over this question. Yes, he is the "Alpha and Omega," the great "I AM," the "Son of Man," the "King of kings and Lord of lords," and the "Savior of the world." But now when I am asked, I am most inclined to say, "Jesus is the one who sits down close to me in my black hole of despair, offering himself until it passes." In some strange way, even though my black hole remains, I'm starting to really know Jesus, and knowing him makes me feel whole.

I guess God knew the best way to help a young boy through a turbulent childhood was to send him a dog. I don't have one now, but it's a running joke in our cul-de-sac how everyone else's dog seems to take a liking to me, including the next-door rottweiler that frightens everyone else. I sometimes wonder what happened to Laddie. I never got a straight answer in seminary whether animals will be in heaven. I hope so.

seven

Don't Mess with the EAMC
(Mr. Adams, ASE Certified)

Institutionalism

I WOULDN'T HAVE MADE IT THIS FAR IN LIFE WITHOUT A
good dictionary. One night, while watching the wacky religious channel (I'm hooked, no psychodrama can top it), one
of the celebrity preachers ranted about church being the last
remaining institution staving off the eradication of Judeo-
Christian values in America. Looking up the word *institution*,
the first definition seemed pretty harmless: "an established
and ordered societal organization dedicated to the public
good." What scared me was the fifth one: "a place of confinement, as a mental asylum."

My primary mode of relating to God and doing Christianity
was something I referred to as "church." The churches I had
been involved in fit the first definition quite well and had an
impressive order to things comparable to the best-run compa-
nies. A baseball diamond identifying the bases (certain spiritual milestones) that must be crossed to reach home plate
(become a model Christian) illustrated nicely the mission of
the church, which was to develop "fully devoted followers of
Christ." An array of services and programs were organized
and offered to meet every need. Several paid staff teams and

77

multiple committees managed the infrastructure of this well-oiled disciple-making machine. It was dedicated to the ultimate public good, the business of saving souls.

I never stopped to ponder or question how my Christianity revolved around church. Jesus instituted the church, and it is all over the New Testament, not to mention a couple thousand years of history. What was there to question, other than which church you were going to? Running with the herd, I was covering all the bases of *fellowship* (Wednesday night small group), *discipleship* (Sunday school), *worship* (Sunday morning service), *ministry* (monthly Strategic Planning Committee meeting), and *evangelism* (Monday night visitation). Somewhere along those bases, my committed church involvement became an adventure in missing the point. Three, sometimes four, times a week I was plugged into some church activity. It was like doing church *was* my relationship with God. Christianity began resembling the minimum-wage jobs I once had; something you did during work hours, but not the kind of thing you brought home with you.

Then one hot, humid day in August with my car's air conditioner on the fritz, my mechanic got me wondering if perhaps that first definition of church as an orderly societal institution might actually produce the confinement and insanity the other definition referred to.

Mr. Ron Adams's small repair shop is on a corner not far from where we live. After earning a BS in mechanical engineering from a local tech school, Ron opened Adams Auto Service sixteen years ago. Given the only thing I know how to do to cars is put gas in them, Mr. Adams has practically become family. God knew I needed an ASE-certified master technician as a friend.

Mrs. Adams answers the phone, greets customers, and does all the paperwork, which mostly is whatever she decides to write down in a spiral notebook. She still uses one of those sliding credit card contraptions and sells cold drinks in cans for fifty cents out of a compact refrigerator. Mr. Adams is always game for a quick oil change on the fly and does many little things at no charge. Mr. Adams will even tell you if and how long you can get by without a car repair if money is an issue. Once, in desperation, we called him at home with a car problem and he didn't mind.

The day before he was going on vacation, I came in with AC problems. Not normally a big talker, Ron was chatty, and we got to talking about how Adams Auto began. He was going on about how much he enjoyed his work when, out of the blue, he remarked how God gave him an interest in and knack with cars and how it was God's way of involving the life of Christ with the lives of all different kinds of people having car trouble. Not the kind of shoptalk I expected from a guy who actually knew what a thermactor bypass solenoid looked like and could tell you your GAWR (gross axle weight rating).

Adams Auto is not listed in the Christian business directory, no fish symbol adorns the front door, and praise music isn't playing in the waiting room. There's not even a Bible verse on Ron's business card. After our little chat, I began paying closer attention to the spiritual aspects of Adams Auto whenever one of our high-maintenance cars brought me around. What would Jesus the mechanic look like? One day I observed it with my own eyes and ears. The one-two punch of Mr. and Mrs. Adams beat any "outreach strategy" church-growth experts could scheme up.

Jingling bells interrupt the quiet waiting room when a flustered young woman blows in the front door of Adams Auto with two small children and a car crisis. More concerned about the woman and her children than the car, Mrs. Adams offers her a seat and comes out from behind the counter. Listening intently as the woman offers more than you want to know in the category of personal life details, Mrs. Adams doesn't miss a beat empathizing with this single mom juggling two jobs and two boys, one with ADD. Ron appears in greasy work overalls, listens to her car story, and heads out the front door to pop the hood.

It dawns on me that this distraught woman in Adams Auto is a mixed bag of need. A spent single mom desperately trying to hold it all together, she feels loads lighter simply by blowing off some steam with someone who cares enough to take time and truly listen. Someone like Mrs. Adams. With only thirty-five minutes to drop her kids off at day care and get to work on time, her practical need for a car repair is urgent. Seeing her crisis, Mr. Adams drops everything he's doing to help her out. She's also going to be standing all afternoon and is grateful for the few moments off her feet in the waiting room. She mentions that this car is the only transportation she has and adds that if a major cost is involved, she's in serious trouble. Thankfully, it's just a belt, and Mr. Adams has her car running before walking back in the front door. Relieved, the woman asks what she owes. Mr. Adams replies, "Don't worry about it. We'll catch you next go-round." She responds with such ecstatic gratitude that you'd think she'd just won the lottery.

Mr. Adams is no dummy, knowing she'll be back next time she needs a car repair. But his motive goes beyond customer retention. He sees his shop as a spiritual post on the potholed journey of life. Pushing through the front door, little did the single mom know a whole other dimension of reality where Christ is present waited. Working weekends and evenings, she couldn't attend church services or midweek small groups, but apparently God knows that and uses nobodies like Mr. and

Mrs. Adams in divine ways. Maybe we all are only a slipped belt away from the kingdom of God. One day your car blows, and suddenly you have Jesus under the hood. To the person driving by, Adams Auto looks like any other mom-and-pop car repair shop. But to that woman, it was an oasis offering care, assistance, rest, mercy, and relationship.

I hope Mr. Adams never reads one of those books describing how insignificant to God secular lines of work are and declaring that what everyone should really be doing is something of greater eternal value, sacrificing occupation, leisure, family, and social involvement to devote more "time, talents, and treasures" to church-related activities or at least something more "ministry" related. Based on my encounters at Adams Auto, perhaps people shouldn't quit their day jobs just yet. Maybe the most convincing invitation to life with God comes from the ordinary Joes. Looking cockeyed at phrases like "incarnational mission," they live each moment of their lives aware of and overflowing with the indwelling life of Christ, providing opportunity for anyone crossing their paths to interact with Jesus in the flesh. Just as people met and interacted with the single fleshly manifestation of Jesus two thousand years ago, maybe the indwelling presence of Christ in all believers provides that ability today in vastly greater numbers. Could that have been what Jesus was referring to when he said, "Anyone who has faith in me . . . will do even greater things than these" (John 14:12 NIV)?

Sometimes I imagine hosting one of those huge church-growth conferences where church leaders pilgrimage to the latest megaministry to hear the star pastor share the latest secret for supersizing their church. As emcee I come out and say, "Okay, let's cut through all the crap. We all know our identities are wrapped up in leading large churches. So go ahead now and turn to the person on your left and right and give them your best estimate of the number (rounding up to the nearest hundred) of people who could feasibly be traced to your church in some form or fashion. If your number is less than two hundred, the Washington Room is set up with round-the-clock prayer partners, grief counselors, and church-growth consultants."

Next, as the music fades and the crowd's buzzing crescendos in anticipation of the megamystery hidden behind the large glimmering gold curtain, a voice captures the auditorium, announcing, "Ladies and gentlemen, please direct your full attention to the stage. Tonight you are going to witness with your own eyes our only hope for saving Christianity in America. Please remain calmly in your seats, silence your cell phones, and put away all image-capturing devices." A few moments later the curtain drops and a collective gasp fills the room. Standing center stage on a platform is a grinning Ron Adams wearing his greasy work overalls and holding a filthy old fuel pump in his hands.

Several large screens roll through the story of his life. At age nine, he's helping out at Uncle Ernie's repair shop. We see him and his high school buddies all covered with oil rebuilding the engine of an old Chevy in his garage. Next we see the trade school he attended in Nashville. We note how elated he is at his first job doing what he loves. Next comes the grand opening of Adams Auto, and we see Mrs. Adams handing out free drinks and popcorn.

The not-so-captivated church leaders become agitated. "What's this?" "Are you kidding me?" There's Ron at the coffee shop, talking about spiritual things with another believer. Hey, it's the guy who operates the wrecker service up the street from Adams Auto. Wait a minute. Two car guys are interested enough in Jesus to willingly discuss him . . . on their own? Shouldn't they be going to church for this sort of thing? Yikes, looks like Ron is taking this whole "indwelling Christ" thing a bit too far! Does he seriously think the risen Christ himself is actually living his life in and through him? That's all well and good, but come on . . . well, I mean, he's a mechanic for crying out loud! Car problems are one thing, but should these people really look to Mr. Adams for spiritual help? Why isn't he giving them a Bible, referring them to a "minister," or recommending a popular Christian book to read?

As the video ends, miffed church leaders are invited to a friendly Q&A session with Mr. Adams. An insistent hand demands the microphone, and it's quickly passed over. "So, Mr. Adams, do you really expect all of us to suppose as part of your ordinary daily interactions in life, people actually encounter the risen Christ through you? My, my, Mr. Adams, tell us where we can find some of that pixie dust that transforms a car mechanic into the Son of God. [The crowd roars in laughter.] Say, let me ask you . . . are you the Christ?"

Amid murmuring voices, Mr. Adams stoops down to speak into the stage microphone. It's awkward for him because he's still holding the fuel pump off to the side so oil doesn't drip all over the stand. "All I can say is Christ lives in me. The life people see me living now is not 'mine,' but his. Christ's Spirit is inside me, and as I know him better, more intimately, his thoughts become my thoughts, his ways my ways, and his love my love. It's his life, so to answer your question, I guess I am Christ."

Another question rings out from the floor: "Mr. Adams, who is the chairperson of the EAMC program at your church?"

He responds, "I'm sorry, the EANC?"

Shocked, the questioner shoots back, "That's EA-*M*-C! Do

you mean to tell me you have been representing Christ independently of the Evangelical Auto Mechanics for Christ?"

He hesitantly replies, "Well . . . uhhh . . . yes."

Outrage ensues. "Blasphemy! What is this going to do to the EAMC?" "Mr. Adams has not received proper training for this. Who does he think he is?" "Next thing you know, Mr. Adams will start claiming he can understand the Bible on his own or doesn't even need one anymore! He already thinks himself Jesus!"

His next interrogator baits him for the incensed mob of purpose-driven pastors. "Mr. Adams, tell us all, where do you attend church?"

Straightening the microphone, he replies, "Well, my church exists all the time, everywhere with everybody. . . . You know, 'where two or three are gathered.'"

The auditorium erupts with "Heretic!" "This man is dangerous! He has no accountability." "How can we grow our churches with loose cannons like this?" "What about biblical teaching and corporate worship?"

Another questioner booms out angrily: "And Mr. Adams, who leads this so-called 'all the time, anyone, anywhere church'?"

Confidently, Mr. Adams responds, "Well, Christ is head of it all, and we listen to and depend on the Spirit to lead and guide us along."

Mayhem seizes the crowd. "Don't you dare throw Jesus and the Spirit in our faces! Do you think for one moment the church could go on without called and trained leaders like us?"

Another chimes in, "Sacrilege! With this mentality, we'll all be out of work!"

A final question is fired: "Hey, Adams, where do you tithe?"

He thinks for a moment and answers, "My money is

God's. The Spirit opens my eyes to the needs around me, and I make my resources available to others as he leads. The joy of giving and the way Christ touches others through me as I become personally involved in their lives is far greater than any tax deduction."

A flurry of angry responses erupts: "How does this fool expect us to keep our programs running?" "I have two daughters in college!" "I'm still paying off my seminary loan!" "This man is an abomination to God and leading our potential church members astray!" "I'm in the middle of a major stewardship campaign. I can't afford this 'Spirit-led' nonsense!" "I'll never break the five-hundred barrier without building a new worship center!" "We must stop him! He can't get away with this!" The throng of mutinous pastors swarm the stage and begin beating Ron Adams with free Sunday school curriculum samples and stoning him with seminar tapes.

Ron is saved by the bell when an announcement comes over the auditorium and breaks up the mayhem: "The Quantum Growth seminar led by Mega Mike starts in five minutes." The crowd disperses, but the whole ordeal is caught on video by the unassuming janitor, who gets a book deal and an appearance on *Larry King Live*.

Okay, maybe I've seen one too many episodes of Jerry Springer, but it never really dawned on me until my experiences at Adams Auto that quite possibly many of the premises of institutional Christianity I had accepted (and perpetuated as a pastor myself) are suspect, given this one cold, hard fact: Christ indiscriminately, fully, and equally establishes his very presence and life within every believer. I know many church leaders who know Christ deeply and serve others selflessly with the purest of motives, so I am not trying to point a finger. However, I have to admit for myself that whenever I conceded to the temptation of deriving my worth from leading a large church or linking my family's financial security to it, I was prone to press people to engage their Christianity primarily in institutional forms: attending services, filling positions, perpetuating programs. This mentality can often be spiritually unhealthy and limit God. I wonder if we have barely begun to realize and scratch the surface of what the risen, living, indwelling Jesus offers to do for us, in us, and through us in the everyday flow of life, work, and relationships.

Waiting on a brake job, the implications began downloading one by one into the operating system of my mind. Whether donning a clerical robe or greasy work overalls, doesn't the one and the same risen Christ in whole and equivalent measure live in you and all believers? Isn't it people God indwells, not buildings? When two or three believers are together encouraging one another in their journey with God, isn't Christ present in their community whether the geographical location is First Baptist, St. Peter's, or Starbucks? Maybe my greatest need isn't another sermon about Christian living, morality, and dos and don'ts. If the life of Christ is configured within me, isn't spiritual growth a matter of grasping the reality of that and being transformed through my intimate, personal, individual relationship with Jesus? And if the risen Christ lives inside all believers, doesn't it stand to reason that significant relationships with one another are another dimension to experiencing Christ's nourishing and renewing presence?

I'm not convinced there's any value added by a large group of believers gathering in one place at one time compared to the benefit of maintaining a few close relationships. I need to hang out and really get to know and experience others depending on the life of Christ in the everyday world of sick kids, control-freak bosses, and the misery of staining and sealing your own deck. I want more than just two Sunday services or a midweek pick-me-up; I want to get to the bottom of Jesus's words: "The kingdom of God is within you." I know what the Bible *says*; I need to understand what it *means* by seeing Jesus in the lives of other believers.

There seems to be this notion that knowing God is a special field of expertise, and "professionals" are needed to sort through the complexities of the Bible and bring order and organization to God's work. Left to ordinary people, who knows what kind of heresy, chaos, and anarchy would ensue. There is a certain human logic to this. If you need surgery, you go to a doctor; if you need legal advice, you call an attorney; if you need your car repaired, you call a mechanic. Likewise, if you need God, you learn to go to church and start doing whatever the leader in the robe, suit, or hip clothes tells you. It makes sense, right? They have the God-degree, spend hours daily in prayer and Bible study, attract crowds who hang on their every word, go off on spiritual retreats—and you don't. Be honest: When in the throes of some theological quagmire, which neighbor comes to mind first? Carpet salesman Carl or Father Francis / Pastor Peter? In every arena there are "professionals" and "amateurs." In Christendom, it breaks down into "clergy" or "staff" (leading) and "laity" or "volunteers" (following).

Yet this didn't seem to be Jesus's logic. My tendency is to project a superior spirituality on people who are either successful organizational leaders, charismatic or gifted public speakers, or intellectually brilliant types. Jesus, however, called attention to the "poor in spirit," the "meek," even the little children, as the most reliable guides for knowing God and his kingdom.

Once while waiting on my car at Adams Auto, I uncovered a *Time* magazine on the table with a cover that read "The 25

Most Influential Evangelicals in America." I quickly turned to the list to see if I was on it. I wasn't. I was probably number twenty-six, but I guess you have to stop somewhere. There were plenty of people with theological degrees, professional ministry positions, or star status within Christendom as mega-leaders, entertainers, or political figures. Mr. Adams wasn't on the list either.

Maybe under the radar, God has left the fate of the world in the hands of the amateurs and a whole lot of divine nobodies. Didn't God himself come as a divine nobody? When it was time to save the world, he stepped down from his heavenly throne, picked up a carpenter's hammer, and went to work. When he chose his team, they were just ordinary people. There's hope for folks like me after all. For most of my adult life, I have been seeking after God in church. Now I'm starting to understand that I'm already wi-fied into the kingdom of God through the Spirit of Christ living in me. Maybe God's coverage is better than Verizon's. Can you hear me now?

eight

....

Pride and Prejudice
(My Gay Friend Richard)

....

Wholeness

A LITTLE AFTER 9:00 A.M. ON SATURDAY, RICHARD TAKES his place in line at Starbucks for his morning fix, a pumpkin spice latte with an extra shot of whipped cream and an oatmeal-cranberry breakfast bar. While waiting, he scans the *New York Times* and local headlines, and suddenly catches something out of the corner of his eye that seizes his attention. Across the room are a teenage boy and a middle-aged man seated in comfy chairs chatting away over their four-dollar coffees. The man is a staff member of the church Richard once attended and the boy, a member of the youth group. They go virtually unnoticed by others in the busy café, just a guy hanging out with some kid on an ordinary run-of-the-mill Saturday morning. Richard sees something more, much more.

Deep in his soul a throbbing sadness rises, leaving him wondering what life would be like if he had been that kid twenty years ago. What would forty look like if some man, any man, had noticed him and wanted to get to know him? While watching, he unravels into a confusing muddle of emotions. He feels jealous of the young man experiencing what he yearned for all

89

his life, the capacity to interact normally and healthily with an adult male.

"Richard, pumpkin spice latte!" calls a voice abruptly. Originally planning to stay, he can't get out quickly enough. Cup in hand, he intentionally backs out the door, stealing a final glance and wishing someone would save him from the hell he's going through. He doesn't want to be homosexual.

Richard and I were friends long before he dropped the bomb. Despite having seen him a couple of days prior, the letter arrived via snail mail, and I was stunned reading his confession. Richard was a caring and giving man with a slightly melancholic personality. But behind the melancholy lay a quirky sense of humor that doubled you over with tears in a heartbeat. Tame and serious-minded accountant by day, he had a creative and animated side most visible onstage as part of the church drama team.

Yikes, my friend Richard was gay? Betrayal, confusion, concern, and embarrassment blew up into a category 5 twister of feelings and emotion. Was I his friend or prospect? I had seen footage of those outrageous gay parades in San Francisco and knew of the evil homosexual agenda to pollute children with their perversion. Now one had infiltrated my circle, posing as a mild-mannered heterosexual interested in Jesus. He even voted Republican! Putting down the letter, I began to ponder, deciding he obviously would need someone (hopefully not me; isn't that what counselors are for?) to hold him accountable for his destructive (read "disgusting") behavior. The least I could do was find one of those rehab programs that miraculously turns gays straight. Maybe we could ship him off to some treatment center and get our old Richard back.

Richard's letter was not a cry for help but a painful farewell. He had suffered long in silence with two equally powerful but seemingly irreconcilable desires. He desperately wanted to know and be known by Jesus, but then there was this deep and confusing hunger to love and be loved by men. This wasn't exactly the kind of "discipleship" issue openly discussed in our Sunday school class, and Richard knew where our church stood on homosexuality. A pamphlet in the church lobby detailed at length our theological beliefs, but what you picked up by hanging around for a while pretty much came down to the following:

1. Jesus is the only way.

2. The Bible is the inerrant Word of God.

3. There won't be any homosexuals in heaven, and they certainly aren't welcome in our little "heaven on earth."

Our church boycotted Disney, signed petitions against gay teachers in public schools, and judged those heretical denominations that sealed their fate with God by accepting gays. In my world there was no such thing as a "gay Christian"; a greedy, gluttonous, hateful, prideful, selfish, lustful, dishonest, hypocritical, vengeful, callous, slanderous, angry Christian maybe, but not gay. God can tolerate only so much and has to draw the line somewhere.

Despite our objections, Richard set out on the perilous path of being a "gay Christian," which meant our new way of "loving" him was to cut off contact until he repented. For the next two years he lived an openly gay life with his Christian live-in partner, Steven. They prayed together and talked about the wonderful love of Jesus, even studied the Bible together. Richard loved and treasured their relationship

91

but silently became increasingly troubled. Jesus was summoning Richard toward something more than his involvement with Steven could provide. Being honest with Steven about his growing doubt concerning their partnership caused great hurt and conflict. Richard finally left the relationship heartbroken and empty.

Miserable, angry with God, and unable to find peace being gay with Jesus, he tried being gay without him. Richard plunged headfirst into the darkness and bondage of gay pornography, adult bookstores, and phone sex. He began meeting dozens of men for meaningless sex. He was trying desperately to . . . well, he wasn't sure. Maybe he was trying to bury the shame of his life or add some kind of meaning in a twisted sort of way. Perhaps he was trying to get someone's attention. Maybe he was trying to connect with something organically male, or perhaps he was trying to blot out the memory of a God he thought had damned him. Could it be that all sin is our doomed attempt to fill the need for God with something besides him?

With each sexual encounter, Richard shook his fist at God, whom he faulted for creating him so deeply defective. How could God have it both ways? Richard didn't believe he had chosen his screwed-up childhood or decided to be a sensitive little boy uninterested in sports or cars. He didn't believe he had chosen homosexuality and the misery it was causing. God needed to heal him or give him the freedom to do what felt natural. God did neither.

Well, in spite of (or because of) his confusion about God, he decided anonymous sex wasn't really working either. Fleeting pleasure gave way to shame upon shame, misery upon misery. So Richard decided he was going to try to conquer his homosexuality with Jesus.

We were elated upon hearing Richard was actually back in a real (heterosexual) church. Joining a Christian group of guys who had come out of the homosexual lifestyle, he attended seminar after seminar, trying to learn the how-to's of rejecting homosexuality and embracing the love of Christ. After all, they told him, he would be okay once he left homosexuality behind. They gave him a foolproof list of dos and don'ts for leaving the lifestyle:

- Don't masturbate.
- Don't check out muscular men you see on the street.
- Don't watch TV.
- Do get a filter for your computer.
- Do journal your feelings.
- Do forgive your father for his absence from your life.
- Do learn how to play basketball or golf.
- Do pray more.
- Do attend church more.
- Do join a Bible study.
- Do call someone when you have a "lust attack."
- Do get an accountability partner or two or three.

Do this . . . do that . . . don't do this . . . don't do that. Richard faintly remembered Christ desiring to know him and wanting to be known by him, but now it all seemed to revolve around stopping his gay behavior.

Following the surefire "seven-step outlines," Richard was supposedly on the tried-and-true path toward recovery (read "heterosexuality"), enabling him to leave homosexuality behind. But things didn't quite go as planned. He experienced a relapse of his old behaviors. The group shunned him and accused him of not really wanting to let go of his sinful behavior and of not having enough faith in God. Others thought he was too rebellious and angry, his will not strong enough to choose truth over lies. Certainly he understood the "conditional acceptance" clause believers and even God himself has for ex-gays. Administered through "loving pressure," acceptance is realized only when sin, habitual or otherwise, ceases to exist and full healing is manifested. The bait-and-switch tendency of evangelical Christianity is curious; it's fine to "come as you are" when you walk the aisle to become a believer, but after that the rules change (at least they do for a select list of behaviors). Seven-step outlines (and subsequent self-flagellation when he failed them) didn't take away Richard's misery or get him any closer to wholeness.

Maybe the healing of homosexuality, or any sin for that matter, isn't found shelved in neat packages of Christian how-to's. Could this be partly because God's idea of healing goes much deeper than mere behavior modification? It seems I keep stumbling into the fact that a spirituality of rules and rituals doesn't fit with the degree of transformation God wants to bring into my life. For Richard, it was an insatiable desire for men; for me, it was an insatiable drive to achieve something spectacular in ministry, but both flow from the same flawed place of seeking to meet a need our own way that only God himself can fill.

Learning to live in dependency on the life of Christ within is a lifelong process, and God does not withhold relationship as a consequence for not yet fully being there. Heck, relationship with God *is* our only hope for change. God made clear that his acceptance of us is secure in Christ so that we would relate to him out of our true, messed-up selves. His motive for our holiness is not to make us less revolting so he can stomach relating to us. We are not capable within ourselves of ever matching God's perfection (which was the whole point of needing a Savior). God's motive for our sharing in his holiness is love; he wants us to experience his wholeness. "Becoming like Jesus" is not merely adopting moral virtues we see in him, but sharing in his completeness that produced them.

Well, for Richard the count was gay with Jesus, strike one; gay without Jesus, strike two; Jesus without being gay, strike three—now what?

I had long since lost track of Richard after receiving his coming-out-of-the-closet letter. Well, that's not being quite honest. The truth is, I couldn't handle having a gay friend and chose to break off contact with him. Meanwhile, the crap of my own life began catching up with me. I was discovering for myself it wasn't going away despite my own lists of dos, don'ts, and fill-in-the-blank discipleship studies. Is the essence of Christianity being "moral"? Does the purpose of God's creating me lie in my behavior? I couldn't find resources within myself to stop destructive patterns of thinking and relating. Day after day, week after week, month after month, year after year, I was a good (albeit tired) Christian, although inside I was the same guy with all the same junk continually longing for wholeness and freedom.

Years later when a letter arrived with a Texas return address, I couldn't think of one soul I knew who lived there. It was Richard. Tears of regret washed down my cheeks as I read his story of tumultuous and failed attempts at dealing with his homosexuality. Maybe having a close male friend or a father-type mentor as a kid would have prevented or disabled Richard's destructive path. Perhaps if I had cared enough, thrown caution and possible embarrassment to the wind, and walked through the crap with Richard two years ago, well, maybe we both would have learned and experienced the freedom and joy of walking in the kingdom of God.

The letter from Texas said:

Dear Jim,

Yes, it's me. Shocked? You'll be disappointed that I'm stuck in basically the same place I was three years ago. Sometimes in the darkness of my aloneness (after I'm halfway through a pack of Salem Ultra Lights), I ask God why I bear the struggle of homosexuality. I sometimes curse him and demand he take it away. He hasn't yet. That makes me very angry. I don't understand. Should I believe what the folks at all the churches have told me: I don't have enough faith, I don't really want to get rid of homosexuality, I don't really want healing. Well, hell, if I didn't really want healing, why would I be so maddened by it all? Why would I sometimes (don't be too freaked out!) consider running my car into an embankment or swallowing a bottle of pills? Why would I have those thoughts if I didn't really want healing??

I admit many times I choose my lust for men over the love of God. I know that doesn't work, but I do it anyway. The thought of having sex with another man or even identifying with guys that do those things is sickening to me. Utterly disgusting! But I still choose to do them. Do you get that? I'm ashamed of myself, and on top of that, every church I've sought healing in ends up ashamed of me as well. I haven't found the answer to the cancer of homosexuality. The "easy" church answers don't work, and I haven't found any other answers, easy or difficult, that work either. I'll shout that loud and clear at the top of my voice to anyone who asks. Why won't God heal me? What is the point? I'm a believer, I'm miserable, and I can't seem to find my way out of the darkness, and all the "pros" of the faith tell me is to "fight the good fight."

I seek Jesus . . . falteringly. I seek real connection with others . . . falteringly. I will tell you it's the hardest thing I have ever had to do. In the process, I smoke too much, I eat too many cookies, and I watch too much Fear Factor. I've stopped going to church. I don't need another fluffy pep talk. Many times I simply can't bear the thought of pasting a phony Jesus grin on my face. I want something real. I NEED something real. I need real people in my life. Where does a guy find people like that? I'm finding non-Christians are more honest with themselves and the struggles of life than Christians. I'm bitter and just can't take it anymore. My parents go to a church where the pastor insists women wear only skirts, no pants. Is that what Christianity is all about, skirts vs. pants?!

I know Jesus is true and real. I just don't know where to start anymore. I've tried so many different things: being a gay Christian, being just gay, being just a Christian. I'm just plumb out of solutions. I know Jesus is the answer, but I don't know where to go to find him anymore. What to do, or not to do. I just don't know.

I will tell you I want so badly to be free. I want people to see me and marvel at the grace of God in my life. I know this is not necessarily the healthiest way to think, but I do! When things are going well and I have a certain amount of celibacy under my belt, I can talk a real good talk. Then life has a way of coming apart at the seams again and off I go, falling into the same old patterns. Then I realize I'm not a success and I'm just plain tired, exhausted really. Life has become one roller-coaster ride after another, and it's making me very miserable, disoriented, and weary.

So, today I start over again. I turn to God, who loves me so very much, and ask to experience his love at the very center of my being. I am becoming more and more convinced healing can only come through the love and life of the Lord Jesus Christ. Perhaps more importantly, healing comes when that love and life are received through the touch of his people. So I've decided to be loved, to receive his love. I need to be open to that. I'm not good at receiving love, because to me, love equals pain, rejection, and betrayal. I need to surround myself with people who may not fully understand my struggle, but love me unconditionally regardless of my past, present, or future behavior. Honestly, I'm not convinced this struggle will ever be totally gone from my life. My hope is that one day I will be a man with the capacity to sit in the corner of a Starbucks and minister my life to another by simply sharing a Saturday morning casual chat and a pumpkin spice latte. Wow. That is the picture of healing.

> *Later,*
> *Richard*

My response back to Richard:

Dear Richard,

Thanks for the letter. It was great hearing from you. I bet you didn't expect one from me either, huh? You would be surprised to know how much I now relate to your struggle. We both long for freedom and wholeness and are deeply disappointed and frustrated with God and ourselves that it isn't coming very easily. My good days are when I know that I know God loves and accepts me as screwed up as I am. This may sound strange, but these days God is telling me to even let go of the "goal of healing" and realize "he" is the goal; knowing him is healing. "He" is what you and I have been looking for all along.

I'm sorry I wasn't a friend ministering the caring touch of Jesus to you, and I ask for your forgiveness. I sometimes wonder how my Christian friends would respond if they knew all the truth about me. I don't quite have your courage in admitting my struggles, but maybe if I did, my friends would too. You may be surprised that over the last couple of years I have learned of two other guys who struggle with homosexuality. I've made my share of jokes about "gay churches" but can't deny I too long for meaningful connection with people who truly accept me in my brokenness and long for something more than behavior modification. Like you, I "want and NEED" something real—real people, real Jesus, not hollow plastic ones.

I was in Starbucks last Saturday and thought of you. My picture of healing is a little different from yours. I imagine myself sitting at a table comfortably chatting and enjoying my java with a close friend struggling with homosexuality. I'm not nervous or embarrassed with plenty of my own crap to worry about. I'm not there to fix him and couldn't hold him "accountable" if I wanted to. We are friends and both know God is what we're looking for. We share where we are on the journey and encourage one another to depend on the love and life of God within us. When it's time to go, we stand and embrace each other. We hold it for a moment and somehow feel the loving presence of Christ with us. As the door closes behind me I feel just a little more whole than when I went in.

Thanks, Richard. I didn't even know it, but God is using you to help me be free. I'm starting to see that sometimes you have to go through hell to get to heaven.

Jim

Like Richard, there are ways I long to be whole and free but am not yet. I'm slowly seeing that God really does love me, although I still sometimes try to earn his love and depend on my talents, achievements, or traits for self-worth. So many times, I choose destructive patterns and misplaced dependencies over his love. I'm weary from my lists of dos and don'ts and tired of trying to figure it out, yet I struggle to simply receive the love and life God wants to give. I understand at the very center of my being Richard's need to experience God's love. If I'm going to get there, I'm going to need some help from a friend or two without conditions and time lines.

nine

Daughters
(Jessica, an American Girl)

Parenthood

THE FROZEN PARTS OF ME BEGAN THAWING AT 8:03 P.M. on April 28, 2000. Somewhere back in my distressed childhood, a thick, icy layer of hurt had formed over my heart. Shutting off my emotions as a survival mechanism growing up, I couldn't seem to turn them back on as an adult. Listening to a grieving friend share deep pain, I'd be nodding my head and offering facial expressions of deep concern but feeling nothing. It was particularly acute in church services as people around me displayed emotions of joy, sometimes tears, while I was going through the motions like a zombie. I understood there were expectations of me in my roles at home, church, and work, and I did my best to fulfill them with or without feeling. God had to find some way to melt the ice and restart the parts of me that had lain dormant for so long. Operation meltdown began unfolding that night in April when Jessica Catherine Palmer was born.

Returning home from the hospital, I never broke 25 mph and crept over bumps and around turns for fear of breaking this fragile thing mummified in blankets and slumping sideways in her car seat. Fearful she was going to slide right out the backseat and through the window, I kept my eyes mostly in the rearview window, frazzling Pam, who gets nervous with my driving even when my eyes are on the road. Parenting is a breeze in the hospital. They do all the work! We held and doted over our newborn, put her on display for family and friends, but when tired or wanting alone time, we rang a buzzer and passed her off to nurses. Oddly enough, there wasn't one of those nifty buzzers at home and no one else to hand Jessica to except each other.

God's parting of the Red Sea seems like a big deal until you experience the miracle of your child sleeping through the night alone in his or her room. Either way, there's really no winning as a new parent. First, you're awake all night with a crying baby, dreaming of the day the child will lie in his or her crib and sleep. Finally, the day arrives when crying gives way to sleep, but then you're awake all night worrying if your baby is still breathing.

Sleep issues with Jessica returned in the toddler phase and kept me on my knees. No, not praying, but crawling out of Jessica's room at night when it was my turn to put her down. After an eternity of rocking and lullabies, I would position her just right in the crib. Lying on the floor next to it until sure she was asleep, I would verrrrry carefully and verrrrry quietly crawl out of the room . . . until my ankle creaked, woke her up, and we had to start all over again. Admittedly, I was a little uptight as a newbie father. My first-year goal was just keeping her alive. This wasn't as easy as you might think. Try navigating one of those three-wheel exercise strollers on garbage day, dodging trash cans and mailboxes. Sleep, sex, and *Monday Night Football* were just a few of the perks of being married without children that were sacrificed, as every ounce of time and energy was now spent holding, feeding, burping, bathing, rocking, wiping, changing, and worrying.

Well, I made it through year one, and she (we) lived on. Jessica is now six years old and full of questions about *everything*. One day while riding together in the car, she asked, "Dad, where does Satan live?" After I babbled off all this stuff about how Satan is a fallen angel and roams around doing no good, it got real quiet for several minutes. Suddenly she said, "Well, I think he lives in Florida." (She might be on to something; there must be some explanation for how the Miami Dolphins have played in recent years.) My explanations didn't fly for other reasons as well. Jessie doesn't understand why God would create a beautiful angel that's so mean. And if Jesus loves everyone so much, doesn't that mean he loves Satan too, and if so, shouldn't we? Will Jesus find some way to win Satan back to God? If not, doesn't that mean there's something stronger than God's love? Well, maybe there are a few questions in there that belong to me as well. I knew I should have paid more attention in my systematic theology class.

I hear many famous authors go to oceanfront bungalows or mountain cabins to write. I wrote most of this book in our little spare bedroom, sitting in the same rocking chair I once sat in to sing Jessica to sleep. Sometimes as I wrote, she'd be stretched out along the bed while I typed away. It's scary how much I love her. Sometimes when she doesn't know it, I'll just sit and quietly study her. Intently coloring her flower, she pauses occasionally to appraise her progress with cocked head and furrowed brow. After sliding her little wisps of golden brown hair behind her ear, she continues on. Eventually she instructs me to close my eyes in preparation for unveiling yet another one of her masterpieces. Soon after, her newest creation is added to the kitchen wall exhibit alongside her gallery of teepees, butterflies, and no-nose, no-neck people with square bodies, little arms, and extremely long legs.

Sometimes when I'm watching her, the levee of emotion inside breaks and my deepest hopes, dreams, and fears for her flood over me. She is an only child, and things about this scare me. It's unbearable to think of her alone in the world when Pam and I are gone. I know just how ruthlessly painful it is, being a grown-up man with an abandoned little boy inside who has never quite recovered. There are people in photographs to whom I ascribe the titles mother, father, sister, and brother, but those titles are hollow and those people are strangers. I have learned to live with a dull despair and sadness lingering just under the surface from knowing I am virtually an orphan despite old pictures I keep tucked away in drawers. There is a certain unsettled and unattached feeling in my soul I don't wish for Jessica, even though it is where I feel closest to Jesus.

Jessica is already picking up on some of her daddy's baggage, and it kills me. I mistakenly thought I did a pretty good job of hiding my obsessive compulsions and fear-based frame of mind. Jessica sometimes looks at me with concern and says, "You're stressed out, aren't you?" and often offers, "Oh, Daaaad, it'll be all right." Not a few nights, I have lain in bed worrying about the collateral damage of my unhealed scars and their affect on her. Once at bedtime after giving Jessica my sermon about overcoming her fears, on the way back to my room, the Spirit pointed out I needed to take some notes myself.

I wish my life were a more complete picture of wholeness and freedom for Jessica to see. Thankfully, I am usually aware of those times when my dysfunction spills out on her. Pulling Jessica aside, I will ask for her forgiveness. The hardest part of talking through it is the dreaded question I ask her about my attitude or behavior: "How did that make you feel?" I sometimes wonder if God uses her answers to break open yet another little part of me so more of him can get in. I know Jessica is aware of my desire and faltering attempts to depend on Jesus for my wholeness. Tending to feel I need to supply her an example of complete healing, maybe she catches glimpses of Jesus in me through all the cracks. I can identify with the Scripture that says, "But we have this treasure in jars of clay. . . ." My hope is in the remainder of the verse, "to show that this all-surpassing power is from God and not from us" (2 Corinthians 4:7 NIV).

Life with Jessica is a roller-coaster ride of emotion; I never know what's coming around the next bend. Unlike me, she doesn't hide her exhilarating joys and painful disappointments. One moment I'm trying to explain why I can't marry her when she grows up and the next, why we can't keep a horse in our one-car garage. Who ever would have thought the same Jim Palmer who is a member of the three-hundred-pound bench-press club would be blubbering at his five-year-old daughter's first flute recital. Okay, maybe you believe she has me wrapped around her finger. All I know is, there is virtually nothing I would trade for our little chats while doing Lite Brite together, not even one of those DirectTV NFL packages. Jessica is softening places in me.

Take, for instance, her fantasy world, something I seemed to lack growing up amid the chaos of my real world. Along with my former church, I contemplated boycotting Disney but instead realized I owed a debt of thanks for the stories I have watched with Jessica that have drawn up water from my deep inner well. One night we all settled into the bed to watch Jessie's very first movie—*The Tigger Movie*. One day

Tigger notices that each of his pals in the Hundred Acre Wood has someone they call family—except him. Deeply troubled by this, Tigger sets off to find his family. Lost, on his own and far from home, he is confronted by the heartbreaking reality there are no other Tiggers to find. Finally, his eyes are opened to realize Pooh, Piglet, Eeyore, Roo, Rabbit, and Owl love him and have been his "family" all along.

Whenever I watch this movie, the scene when Tigger realizes he's alone in the world punctures something inside, and an overpowering sadness pulsates within me. My soul identifies with Tigger's unfulfilled longing to belong to a family. The story stirs up painful places left behind and the agonizing disconnect I carry in life. Once when I was watching the movie by myself, Jesus conveyed he understood my lonely, disconnected place and what it was like to be unwanted and abandoned. Tigger's story seemed to open up this place Jesus wanted into. He lifted the lid off this buried hurt to share my sadness. He spoke of desiring deep connection with me. I'd probably heard a hundred sermons about how Jesus "sympathizes" with my humanness and was "a man of sorrows," but somehow it was necessary for me to go to the Hundred Acre Wood to experience him with my heart. Like Tigger, I've been secretly holding out for what I will never find. Other than Pam and Jessica, there simply aren't any Palmers I will ever truly know as family. But maybe it's been right before my eyes and I've missed it; God himself is the Father, Mother, Sister, and Brother I most want and need.

Jessica once brought home from the library a few CDs filled with songs from several Disney movies. Many of these songs had a similar effect in stirring hidden places deep inside, becoming touch-points with God. The lyrics of "Go the Distance," sung by Hercules in the 1997 animated movie, uncovers an unspoken dream of mine, achieving something great to finally find my place or at least erase all doubt I should be here. I know exactly what Hercules wants when he sings of "a far-off place where a great warm welcome will be waiting for me, where the crowds will cheer when they see my face and a voice keeps saying this is where I'm meant to be." As he sings, I am faced with shameful feelings of inadequacy and the burden of becoming a somebody. Meeting me there, Jesus says he accepts me as I am with nothing to prove.

Recently Jessica has become attached to *The Princess and the Pauper* characters and story. We purchased the DVD, which also came with a bonus CD containing all the songs from the movie. Dancing and performing the songs with Jessica in the front room, we take turns alternating who's the princess and who's the pauper. (Let's just keep that our little secret.) The irony of the movie is how the pauper longs for freedom, which she imagines is possible only through the kind of fame and fortune the princess has. Yet, this very wealth and status have become a ball and chain to the princess. In the song titled "Free," the princess sings, "What would it be like to be free? You would think that I'm so lucky that I have so many things. I'm realizing every present comes with strings. But I'll never stop believing there's more to living than gloves and gowns. In my dreams, I'll be free."

Acting out the part, the realization of just how lifelike the plot is became clearer. I was carrying around my own "if only" scenarios I was convinced would make my life complete. Truth is, I wouldn't mind having a little of that fame and fortune myself. When Jessica was born, I was hot on the trail of making a big splash in Christendom but, like the princess, was finding there were strings attached and a price to pay. Even as a pastor, if your claim to fame is being an awesome speaker (which mine was), you're still only as good as your last sermon, which becomes a ball and chain. Just the smallest criticism of a sermon crushed me. Sometimes I wondered if people were drawn to me for who I really was or just because I could mesmerize an audience of people with my speaking gift. I was wondering, right alongside the princess, what it would be like to be free, free from the need to be spectacular, free from my addiction to people's applause, free from the burden of being a somebody.

Somehow, the story stirred a desire within me for something more than what fleeting human praise and admiration could provide. Even all my religious activity couldn't satisfy this, wearing me out further. Strangely, *The Princess and the Pauper* story was a mirror showing me how futile my strategy was to find significance, meaning, and worth in achievement and recognition. One rendering of Jesus's words in the Gospel of Matthew reads, "Are you tired? Worn out? Burned out on religion? Come to me. Get away with me and you'll recover your life. . . . Keep company with me and you'll learn to live freely and lightly" (Matthew 11:28–30 MSG). I guess we have to get to the end of our striving in order to receive the freedom Jesus wants to give.

Jessica's imaginary stories were getting through to me. Somehow what I was missing in sermons and fill-in-the-blank study guides was being expressed through talking donkeys, nannies that rode umbrellas, and beasts that married up. (I won't even get into the Muppets.) I guess God can use anything to draw us to himself. Of course, Disney movies don't always make good theology, but then again, sometimes I wonder if maybe we should start busing people into the Magic Kingdom in an effort to recover a sense of imagination for that other kingdom Jesus spoke so much about.

The last couple of years, Jessica has become interested in the American Girl dolls and book series. Each doll has a series of books, essentially stories of young girls learning life's lessons and coming of age. I think I'm coming of age myself right along with her. There are parts of me that somehow were stunted by the hurts of life back there as a little boy. I guess Jessica and I in some ways are growing up together. Maybe you really can be born again. Little by little I'm being broken into life.

A day is probably coming when Jessica will survive me. In case that day comes sooner than expected, I decided to write Jessie the following letter. It brings me peace to know she can always find it in this book.

Dear Jessie,

One day you're going to be reading this letter and I'll be gone. You're six right now, but I didn't want to get caught in one of those things where you put off something that's real important to you and then it's too late. I know you know this, but I hope whenever you read this letter you will feel all over again how much I love you. Out of everything that happened during my stay on planet Earth, I'm not sure it ever got any better than our front room hoedowns, those first-one-to-the-bed races (which somehow you always won), and our search-and-rescue missions with your bed as the boat at sea saving all the drowning stuffed animals on your floor.

I am so thankful that God enabled me to see the gift you were to me. I knew so many people through life who seemed to always be chasing something, which distracted them from the treasure right beneath their nose. There's a lot of things I didn't get quite right, but I never wandered too far from

*knowing the finest place on earth was at home eating choco-
late pudding pie and playing Sorry with you and Mom. YOU
brought me such happiness just because of who YOU are. It
wasn't anything you did; it was everything you did. Do you
see? It was you, Jessie. I'm going to need at least a few thousand years in eternity to thank God for making me your dad.*

*Over the course of my life, I traveled to some of the most
remote and far-off places on earth. Sometimes you cover thou-
sands of miles to get to where you're going. It took awhile for
me to figure out the journey to God is a matter of eighteen
inches. It doesn't sound like much, but I'm quite sure I never
would have gone the distance if you hadn't shown up.
Somehow, someway, somewhere, I got all turned around, and
God became a head-thing. I was going through the motions
terribly empty and worn out inside. Just south of my head was
my heart, but it wasn't really working and couldn't make any
connection to him. I was "saved" but lost, busy but barren.*

*Then God sent you, and little by little I began to discover
the Jim buried deep below. It scared me, Jessie. You brought
out a range and depth of feelings I never knew were in me. I
went from being a middle linebacker to a guy needing tissue
during a Kodak commercial. God used your wide-open, free,
spontaneous, unpretentious heart to awaken the same in me.
Somehow, along the way of mending your hurts and disappointments and cheering your thrills and triumphs, my heart
was mending as well.*

*When I discovered the once frozen river of emotion deep
within me, I also found God there—or maybe it's that he
found me. Turns out he wanted to know the real Jim and had
little use for the religiously simulated, spiritually synthetic,
church-automated one I assumed he wanted. Jessie, thanks
for lending me a hand. Don't ever lose your heart. When life*

hurts, Jesus will be with you there. It's not always easy living from your heart, but take it from Dad, any other way is not really living. So when you travel down to your heart, I hope you will hear my voice reminding you what a precious treasure you are, and I will be planning a huge "My Little Pony" party for our reunion. See you soon.

Always and Forever,
Dad

P.S. I'll ask Jesus about the whole mermaid thing.

I used to be afraid of my heart, partly because my religion told me it was bad and partly because the hurt locked deep within it was too overpowering to face. Over these past six years with Jessica, my deepest disappointments, greatest fears, and secret dreams have been slowly seeping out and becoming less threatening. True, the Bible says, "The heart is deceitful," but the Bible's shortest verse should not be overlooked: "Jesus wept." For a long time I fit God's description of people who were busy with religious things but whose "hearts [were] far from me." You have to first find your heart if you ever expect it to beat with the pulse of God. The Tin Man eventually found his. I'm finding I have one too.

ten

August 7, 1959–July 22, 2000 (Father of Four)

Belief

HANGING OUT WITH FAMILY ON A WARM SUMMER MORNING, Bill thinks to himself, *It just doesn't get any better than this.* A gentle breeze rolls in from surrounding pastures, offsetting the rising July heat. Bill and his nine-year-old twins are tackling a few chores in the barn. Bill's brother Steven and family stop by, prompting the kids to scheme of escaping to a four-wheeler adventure. Carol Ann, college sweetheart and wife of sixteen years, saunters by on horseback with four-year-old Sarah Kate riding shotgun. The only one missing is fifteen-year-old Jessica, who is pursuing her passion of helping others on a mission trip in Mexico. A surge of gratitude sweeps over Bill for the family he loves. He winks at Carol Ann and waves to Sarah Kate with her broad toothless grin as they trot off for a morning ride. Beginning as a picture-perfect day, it would soon unravel into a nightmare, changing the Lee family forever.

A while later, the kids are off riding somewhere, and Bill returns to the barn to finish up. Putting away some tools, he hears a faint crying off in the distance. He stops to listen closely; though barely audible, it most definitely is someone screaming. Bill yells to his brother outside the barn, "Steven, do you see Sarah Kate in the pasture?"

"Yes," he replies.

"Is she alone?"

"Yes."

Dropping the tools, Bill hurries to his truck and screeches off. Homing in to the crying, he finds Sara Kate wandering in the field, crying uncontrollably. The horse and Carol Ann are nowhere to be seen. Panicked, Bill asks, "Sara Kate, is Mommy okay?"

"Noooooowwwaaah!"

At that, Bill looks up and sees the horse in the next field over.

Bill races out to the horse and finds Carol Ann facedown on the ground, motionless. Turning over her limp body, she appears dead, blood trickling out of the corner of her mouth. Bill finds no pulse and immediately tries mouth-to-mouth and CPR. By happenstance, nine-year-old Caleb tools by on his four-wheeler. Bill, who is by now covered in blood, turns and yells for Caleb to hurry home and call 911. Forty-five agonizing minutes go by before Life-Flight arrives, leaving Bill holding his unconscious wife and sinking into a darkness from which he might never again emerge as a sane, normal, believing man.

Piecing together the story from Sarah Kate, Bill learns that Carol Ann had eased the horse into a steady gallop when the horse tripped and stumbled, slamming them hard to the ground. Carol Ann, unconscious, was still attached to her stirrup when the horse arose from the fall and took off again, dragging her a good hundred yards.

Initial reports inspire optimism she might regain consciousness, but on day three hope teeters on a string and is ultimately lost as doctors inform Bill, who has not moved from Carol

Ann's bedside, she probably will not make it through the night. Arriving home after midnight, exhausted physically and emotionally, he relays the news to daughter Jessica, evoking grief that awakens one child after another. Soon the whole family holds one another on the kitchen floor, paralyzed by the news that Mommy might not be coming home . . . ever. Shock gives way to the late hour, and each cries themselves to sleep, or so Bill thinks.

At 4:00 a.m. Caleb, still awake, quietly calls out in the darkness, "Daddy, I don't think I'm going to make it."

"What do you mean?" Bill asks.

He explains, "I feel scared and alone, like in the woods, in the dark, and no one is coming."

Tuesday morning, July 22, 2000, Bill sits at Carol Ann's bedside in the intensive care unit. With the three youngest at Grandmother's house and teenage Jessica in shock on a waiting room couch, I pace the hall while downing my fourth cup of coffee. Memories of my friendship with Bill roll across the screen of my mind. Our paths crossed through mutual concern for at-risk youth. As the newly appointed executive director of a nonprofit inner-city agency for abused and abandoned children, I was exploring vocational paths for older kids, most of whom would never finish high school. Bill, a successful CEO of a regional HVAC and mechanical contracting firm, actively involved both personal and company resources in community initiatives aimed at helping troubled youth.

We first met to discuss the idea of pairing our older teens with his employees to learn the plumbing trade. That year we honored Bill as Volunteer of the Year at our annual city-wide dinner. We hit it off and in time became personal friends. Over coffee at a nearby café, we shared our lives and spiritual journeys. A humble and giving person, Bill lived out his Christianity without pomp or circumstance. He also had the dubious privilege of listening to my latest harebrained idea of the next great megathing I was going to do for God. He would sit there patiently while it became painfully obvious how ludicrous my schemes were, which sometimes didn't hit me until I heard myself justifying them to a stable individual. God used him to spare the world (and me) of much stupidity.

My friend is now waiting, praying, and hoping for the miraculous. A flood of questions washes over me. *Why? Why Bill? Why Carol Ann? Why these children? How can God allow this? It makes no sense. How can anything good possibly come from this?*

Bill is told there isn't much time. He takes Carol Ann's hands and says his long good-bye as she slips from coma into death. He cannot bring himself to let go, but must; four motherless kids now look solely to him. Permanently recorded in my soul is my encounter with Bill moments later. Jessica, vacant yet clinging to his side, we embrace tightly for what seems like minutes without words, for even the mention of God feels scandalous to me.

In the hours and days following Carol Ann's death, shock gives way to unspeakable agony. Deafening memories of landing helicopters, screaming sirens, wailing children, and the vision of Carol Ann lying bloody on the ground bring torment and nausea. Well-intentioned friends demand retelling the story of misery and loss. Slammed by a blizzard of pain and desperate for relief, Bill is now planning Carol Ann's memorial service and making burial arrangements. The constant dribble of conversation around him at the funeral home seems surreal. Lying with his wife in bed just days earlier, Bill now privately spends a final few minutes at the casket, reaching in to touch Carol Ann one last time. As she is lowered into the ground at the grave site, Bill has no idea the depths of suffering to which he will yet descend.

In addition to being company CEO, Bill was now leading an adolescent M.A.S.H. unit on the front lines of a world that callously kept spinning with or without wife and mother. Sometimes grief arrived spontaneously, unconcerned with interrupting business meetings, phone calls, or even the smallest task. The gaping hole left inside would not be denied.

Night after night, the family wept and slept together on the floor, dreading another morning that would begin another day of pain. And yet it would come, forcing them from sleep into their living nightmare. Life with four struggling kids, schools, doctors, sports, groceries, programs, and friends brought chaos. Responsibilities at home and work accumulated like trash on a vacant lot, threatening to push Bill toward collapse. In the darkness, he would sink into his favorite chair exhausted, anguished, and wondering if he could survive another day.

As weeks turned into months, Bill longed for the time when the sorrow had been fresh and tears came easily. The emotional release would have lifted the burden, if only for a while. The constant reminders of Carol Ann and their life together unbearably filled every room and acre. Sometimes Bill would awaken at night or walk inside after work and instinctively call for Carol Ann, forcing the agony of her absence upon him. Yet the loss of Carol Ann would soon be pushed to the sidelines as another tragedy and near loss struck.

Having lunch with Bill, I listened as he shared with me how thankful he was for the way his teenage daughter, Jessica, was coping. The very next day, Bill received an urgent call at his office telling him Jessica had attempted suicide at home by shooting herself in the head. Bill remembers after the call lying down on the floor in his office, feeling he could not take any more.

I need to stop here and talk with you, the reader, about this chapter. It was the most difficult for me in writing this book. After completing the first draft, I sent it to Bill for feedback. Everything you've read up to this point was in that draft, and Bill agreed that it expressed, as much as a few paragraphs of words are capable, the devastation and agony of Carol Ann's tragic death. The first draft then continued, delving into the issue of why God allows suffering.

I was starting to personally know many believers with similar stories of tragic loss, which disturbed me. Maybe I was next. Was anything of mine safe in God's hands? Who's to say I wasn't a phone call away from discovering my Pam and Jessica had died in a car accident? Tragedies of every scale happen every day all over the world, but when they began taking out my close friends, a frightening truth buried beneath my handy illusions of God clawed its way to the surface of my soul. I am vulnerable to loss and suffering, and knowing God doesn't change that. So . . . do I really want to know *that* God? If God is not there to protect me, and if accepting Christ, doing church, being good, and obeying aren't paying into some divine insurance policy to take care of me, at least with some minimal coverage, then what is this all about anyway? If I can lose my family, my job, my health, and my dignity, then what good are God and this life of sacrifice?

Though Bill concurred with my descriptions of his pain, he was shocked by how I failed to mention all the ways God's grace factored in—the grace he and his family experienced beginning the very moment he found Carol Ann facedown in the field and continuing to this day. Bill shared with me countless ways God was present with him and his family, some of them unfathomable. I must admit that as he expressed these things, I doubted. To this day, there's still a part of me that struggles to believe. Unaware at the time, my selective memories edited out this side of Bill's story. I now see it was an unconscious expression of my own skepticism. It's easy to reject something you simply don't understand. What follows are a few glimpses of that thread of hope mysteriously woven throughout Bill's and his family's pain and suffering, making the remainder of this chapter a substantial departure from the original draft.

I must warn you, the following things you are about to read, which I either encountered directly or was told by Bill, I do not pretend to fully understand. I am falteringly assigning words and sentences to describe realities beyond my own comprehension.

Two weeks prior to Carol Ann's death, they took a family vacation to Yellowstone National Park. Having some time to themselves, Bill and Carol Ann decided to go exploring. As they crossed a narrow pass in the hills, Carol Ann spotted a herd of mountain goats. Bill had long had a fascination with mountain goats, and they pulled over to take a closer look. Back in the car, Carol Ann remembered once coming upon a verse in the Bible about mountain goats. Intrigued, Bill asked her to find it, which she eventually did, in the Old Testament book of Job. The book opens with a horrific scene where God-loving Job loses everything in a tsunami of catastrophic loss, including his children, home, possessions, and health. In the next several chapters, Job's "friends" are embroiled in trying to explain why all this happened, and though they are wide off the mark, Job regrettably starts buying into it. Finally, in chapter 38, God steps in, silencing everyone, and speaks directly to Job. Essentially telling him to quit trying to figure it out, God builds an impressive case with a litany of questions designed to show Job he is big enough to be trusted despite the absence of an acceptable human explanation. In Job 39:1 God asks, "Do you know when the mountain goats give birth?" (NIV). Point being, our understanding is vastly overestimated in comparison to the One who possesses all understanding and knowledge.

After Carol Ann read the verse, the two of them began to discuss where each was at in their spiritual journey. Bill shared how after many years of being a believer, it seemed he was just beginning to appreciate the immensity of God. Carol Ann shared her belief that God's intentions for their family were immeasurably more than anything they could ever imagine. Holding hands, they continued the picturesque drive just happy to be together, marveling at the beauty of creation and worshipping the Creator. The memory of this conversation and Bible verse came to Bill's mind while at Carol Ann's bedside during the last remaining moments of her life. Though in a coma, Carol Ann, doctors explained, was still capable of hearing, so Bill turned to chapter 39 of Job and began reading, "Do you know when the mountain goats give birth?" Before beginning verse 2, God made his presence known to Bill. Revealing himself as the God who never changes, he impressed upon Bill once again his immensity and reminded Bill of the unimaginable intentions pondered during that glorious and special drive with Carol Ann, which were no less true at that moment as she slowly drifted away. God was telling Bill he was present whether it was the best or worst day of his life.

Overcome by this divine exchange, Bill muttered, "Oh, my God. He's real. The drive, the mountain goats, Job 39:1 . . .

he has known all along. God knew then and he is here now. Somehow I'm going to get through this." Standing before his deceased wife, Bill remembers thinking as horrific, disorienting, and unexplainable as it all was, he at least had a mustard seed of faith to say God is real; he is present and is bigger than all of this. In the days, weeks, and months ahead, this proved to be the seed God watered, pruned, and doted upon to grow a tree of shelter and hope in Bill's life. Though not softening the agony of losing Carol Ann, the recurring experience and assurance of God's presence sustained Bill and each of his children in the days ahead, indeed proving, beyond comprehension, that God continued being present in Bill's life and manifesting himself in sometimes supernatural ways.

The day after Carol Ann's death, four-year-old Sarah Kate told Bill before going to bed that moments before the accident, God told her something terrible was about to happen. To this day, Sarah Kate knows deep within that God was present before the fall that changed her life forever. One evening weeks later, Caleb, who had been refusing discussions about Mom living in heaven, came downstairs with eyes as big as saucers and shared how he talked with an angel. While upstairs in his room, he had looked down into the backyard of their secluded farm and had spotted a mysterious homeless-looking man standing by a tree. After watching him awhile, Caleb knocked on the window, prompting the man to fly up to the second story and peer at Caleb through the glass. He told Caleb, "God is here with you, and you will be okay."

Even Bill, on the night Caleb described being alone in the woods with no one coming for him, recalls two things vividly. Lying beside Caleb on the floor, he was struck with how his son's description surprisingly captured exactly how he himself felt. The very next moment, an intense awareness of

121

God's presence swept over him, letting Bill know he was in fact not alone and "Jesus is coming." Though he mentioned these exact words to me several times, frankly I thought the whole "Jesus is coming" thing was strange. Coming where? Coming how? Coming why? Wasn't Jesus technically already *there*, indwelling Bill?

Sometimes hope came through very unassuming means. Caleb's more reserved twin brother, Jacob, never saw angels or heard a voice from God. Yet one of the underlying threads of hope was how Jacob seemed certain, quietly certain, that they would be okay. Less reactive than the others in his response, his quiet assurance was at times a source of calm for Bill.

When getting together, Bill often talked about God "showing up." Curiously, these experiences of God's presence were immensely meaningful even though his grief and anguish continued. This is just one of several paradoxes that did not compute. How can suffering and healing, brokenness and wholeness, despair and hope coexist? Wasn't God supposed to ease people's pain in trials? Bill insisted he was not angry with God. This was maddening. In disbelief, I would often think, *Come on, Bill. Be real. She's not even my wife, and* I'm *angry and disillusioned with God.* In the first draft of this chapter, imagining all the horrors, I had Bill in deep depression contemplating suicide, feeling betrayed and abandoned by God, wondering how God could kill his wife of sixteen years, and stumbling along with no reason for living except the children.

After reading the first draft, Bill's response by e-mail included the following remarks:

As I read the draft, I found myself feeling like some of it wasn't really the way I felt. I would say that I never wanted to die. I only wanted for it all to go away. And it seems incomplete to say that only my kids and my habit of living are what kept me alive. There was a sense there was more to it than I could see. There was surely hope for living that kept me going, some certainty that this was not the end, that there was a picture I couldn't see. God would not abandon me there, alone. There was some unexplainable trust driving me to get up and make that painful cup of coffee for one.

Later on you talked about acute depression. I wouldn't use that phrase. I never felt deep depression, only deep anguish. And finally, in the next to last paragraph, I would have to say your questions outlined were really not questions I had. I know you are trying not to have pat Christian answers to hard questions in circumstances like these, but somehow, I never really wondered, for example, if God killed Carol Ann. I wondered why he allowed it, but I always knew there was some reason I would never know and didn't care to know really. His ways were beyond my understanding, and I knew it. I always knew he was good, just that my circumstances were not, and reconciling that was difficult. I remember early on, rarely feeling abandoned, often feeling his presence, but at the same time feeling deep pain, which again was difficult to reconcile. I wasn't angry, just very confused. There is a big difference, and I couldn't really own the words of that paragraph.

In the weeks and months following Carol Ann's death, I poked and prodded, trying to figure out what Bill was doing to have such hope and confidence in God. Was it his prayer life or time spent immersed in God's Word? For me this was by far the most baffling and vexing aspect of Bill's journey into the night. I remember Bill saying at one point in the hospital that he was too weary to even pray for Carol Ann. A friend of his kindly instructed him that the only thing God needed Bill to do was simply take his next breath, then the next, and the next. What kind of counsel was that? Didn't Bill at least need to meet God halfway? What about seeing a counselor or reading a Christian book about suffering?

I do not know what to make of Bill consistently saying God did everything and Bill did nothing. How was that possible? Isn't that overstating it? Surely, Bill was doing *something*. As I pressed him further, the only thing he would own up to was choosing to believe and trust with his mustard seed of faith. This was a leap for me, not familiar with a God who doesn't require or need me to do my thing in order for him to do his. Apparently, God has the prerogative of freely supplying his children what they need independently of what they do or don't do. During one period, Bill went weeks without opening his Bible, but God just kept on "showing up" and Bill just went on trusting—grieving, fulfilling responsibilities at work and home, hurting, caring for each of his children, weeping, but always trusting.

Jesus was once asked, "What must we do to do the works God requires?" Jesus answered, "The work of God is this: to believe in the one he has sent." Maybe this is what was meant by those words spoken to Bill on the floor next to Caleb, "Jesus is coming." Yes, the risen Christ already resided inside Bill, but now Christ's presence within was going to be sufficient for Bill in ways he had never experienced before, and Bill could trust and depend on him. Walking through the darkness, there would be hope, peace, and life for Bill because Jesus himself is all these things and more, and Jesus was there with him. There was nothing for Bill to do but believe. I guess God's grace really is an "amazing" grace after all.

I sat in church for years surrounded by creeds, stained-glass portraits, and hymns about Jesus, but the Jesus Bill was showing me was real beyond anything I had ever imagined or thought possible. As Bill's journey was unfolding before my eyes, Christ was reassuring me that he is enough for whatever comes my way.

I can now see why at times I seemed more devastated by Bill's ordeal than even Bill was. I could not imagine Christ being sufficient in the midst of such catastrophic loss, precisely because it was *his* loss and not mine. I could not walk in Bill's shoes to truly know the agony of his tragedy; neither could I know the unique ways Christ was helping him. Perhaps what God most wanted me to come to grips with in Bill's suffering was trusting God's sufficiency for others.

As a young boy, I accepted responsibility for my mother's depression and tried hard to compensate for it. This proved to be a self-destructive pattern I would carry into adulthood. If the people closest to me were unhappy or dissatisfied with life, I automatically blamed myself and tried to fix it. As a pastor, the feeling of being needed by others who depended on me as a source of truth and counsel became an addiction. But like any addictive drug, the downside soon eclipsed the benefit, and accepting an overinflated role of significance in people's lives was depleting my inner reserves of strength to dangerously low levels.

Though I know this must sound ridiculously rudimentary, Bill's story forced me to come to grips with the fact that there is only one Savior and another one isn't needed. This understanding has birthed in me the freedom to come alongside others to share their burdens without trying to rescue them. There are times when I'm listening to a person share a hurt or struggle, and no flash of insight or guidance comes to mind. At one time in situations like this, I would have forced myself to come up with something, but now I recognize that often it's the Spirit wanting me to keep my mouth shut and simply offer the ministry of presence and listening. My natural instinct is to jump in and try to save someone I see drowning, but sometimes a person needs to sink to rock bottom in order to find God. Whether it's Pam, Jessica, a close friend, or someone I meet on the street, Christ is who they need, and I can best serve others by pointing them in his direction.

Bill and I met for coffee during the week marking the five-year anniversary of Carol Ann's death. Checking e-mail several weeks later, I noticed one from Bill in my in-box. This is how it read:

It has been five years; sometimes feeling like five days, sometimes, five decades. Some days I can still hear her laugh, feel the touch of her hair. Every day I think of her. The struggle of moving on in life without Carol Ann has been bittersweet, first more bitter, giving way to a sweetness I now know I never knew before. I have learned the degree to which a man experiences brokenness is the same degree to which he can experience wholeness. Out of the depth of my pain, I have been privileged to feel a new height of hope. I realize for the first time the true brevity of life, and yet for the first time understand its intense value. I am a deeper, richer, more purposeful man than ever before. I have tested my God and found him trustworthy. Oh, I find days of fear, doubt, and pain. But I have found more days of courage, certainty, and healing. Some days I feel I know less about God than I ever realized, yet I know him more intimately than I ever imagined possible. I recently sat at Carol Ann's grave and wondered what she must have been doing that day. As I pondered, I realized there are but a few things that matter to her now. And there will be but a few things that will matter to me then. And thus there are but a few things that matter to me today: to know him, and make him known.

Bill's daughter Jessica has come a long way since attempting suicide and is now a junior in college. After reading the chapter, she shared some of her own thoughts:

As the years go by, I begin to understand more fully the grace God has shown my family. I never believed our complete joy could be restored after such a tragic loss. The pain of losing my mother and experiencing dark depression, which led to self-destructive actions, did not destroy me or us. Through these circumstances, God has begun a new work in me. I sense his strong calling on my life and see his redemptive power in even the darkest of situations. His glory has been magnified through all he has done in my life. Even on days when I don't understand his plan, I still know beyond a shadow of a doubt he is all powerful and all loving, and as surely as the sun rises, he will remain faithful.

While home on break, Jessica and Bill are in the car by themselves. Flipping through a magazine, Jessica talks a mile a minute about classes, friends, and other goings-on at school. Caught by something interesting on the page, she becomes quiet, giving it her full attention. Bill eventually breaks the silence. "Jessica, can I ask you something?"

Sensing her dad's somberness, she closes the magazine and replies, "Of course, Dad." Pondering the words, she prompts him again. "Dad?"

The question finally comes. "Jessica, do you ever get the

strange feeling that even with all the tragedy and suffering we have gone through, it seems something very good is happening to us?"

Staring straight ahead, Jessica absorbs her dad's question, which brings a slow trickle of tears down her face. "It's true, Dad. . . . I'll always love Mom, but I feel it too, and I'm so glad you said it. . . . Something good is happening."

At first it discouraged me that I was so skeptical of Bill's experience with God in his suffering. Now I see, God is there even if I cannot feel or quite trust that presence. Maybe God is not offended by human doubt and fear but longs to help us and, more important, is able to help us. It's strange how God works. Bill told me this chapter is bringing an added measure of healing to each of his kids and is a "personal treasure" for his family. I see more clearly now why God allowed me to stand on the edge of Bill's journey through darkness, and I can feel my own mustard seed of faith growing. My own question has been answered: Yes, I want to know *that* God.

eleven

(E) None of the Above
(Jill, the Flaming Swim Teacher)

Politics

I VOTED FOR JOHN KERRY. . . .

Half of you are now aghast, searching for the nearest incendiary device to set fire to this book.

Hold on.

I really voted for W. . . .

Now the previously smug are shaking their heads in disgust, wondering why the government doesn't put parental-control labels on Republican-authored books.

Those of you who are third-party people are appalled I would consider voting for either.

How about this: Half of you can believe I voted for Kerry, the other half I voted for Bush, the rest of you, well, Ralph Nader—and we can all be friends.

Republican, Democrat, Libertarian, conservative, liberal, moderate; to be honest, I'm not sure what I am. If asked on a multiple-choice test, I would mark both "(d) all of the above" and "(e) none of the above." Back when ignorance was bliss, I used labels to sort out the good guys from the bad. For example, Southern Republican Protestants ("us") desired to save America while Northern Democratic Catholics ("them") lived to dismantle it. A day did come (or maybe it was many days) when circumstances forced my hand and I had to give credit where credit was due. Up in the North, the blue states started turning out world championship sports teams—the New England Patriots, the Boston Red Sox, the Chicago White Sox. Democrats championed social justice and the environment, and the Catholic pope John Paul served as a powerful symbol of Christian peace and courage throughout the world. Despite my biases, these blue-state people sure seemed pretty impressive. So impressive that I decided to join them.

I became "progressive," which meant becoming more or less "them," making the old "us" the new "them" (confused yet?). With my more enlightened view, I looked down my nose on those simpleton, fundamentalist, capitalist barbarians until discovering my newfound open-mindedness had glitches too. Whether Michael Savage or Michael Moore, in the end disillusionment reigned, as people and life scenarios I encountered proved contradictory to the assumptions of both my conservative and liberal spins. It was maddening that whichever political ideology I assumed, there were plenty of situations that poked holes through it.

Just when I thought all societal ills flowed from heartless millionaires thinking more of decorating their yachts than helping the homeless, I met some giving large percentages of their fortunes to people in need while employing significant numbers of those I claimed they didn't care about. Convinced most welfare recipients were working the system, buying beer and cigarettes with food stamps, I encountered some single moms, unable to make it on minimum wage, attending school at night to better themselves, and strictly following a personal budget, all the while still coming up short. Assuming all Middle Eastern Muslims were jihad-happy, America-hating extremists, I became friends with some who denounce violence, love America, and pray with me even though they know I worship Jesus. Pretty soon I expected to find a foursome of NRA and PETA executives playing eighteen holes at Martha's Vineyard. (Okay, maybe hell hasn't frozen over yet.)

For crying out loud, would someone just tell me who to hate and pin the world's problems on? People who previously fit into my "I'm-excused-from-loving-you box" were not cooperating very nicely. Sure, there are greedy wealthy people, folks who abuse the system, and wackos who want to see it all go up in flames, but mostly I found my stereotypes didn't accurately describe the ordinary people I knew. It just didn't pay to let others do my thinking for me. As a proud conservative, I'm sure Rush and Sean did their homework and were right about many things, but slowly I realized you can't presume much about another person without actually getting to know him or her. Talk radio is a dangerous place from which to view the world.

To imply these realizations resulted from some determination within myself to assign all people equal dignity is a far cry from the truth. No, that would be Gandhi. Labeling people was actually very comforting. It supplied what every adolescent adult like me needed: scapegoats to blame, adversaries to defeat, and dimwits to set straight, making me innocent, victorious, and right. I'd still be pasting labels on everyone today if I hadn't been set straight myself by my six-year-old daughter's swim teacher.

Signing up Jessica for private swim lessons, Pam and I decided I would take her each week as a daddy-daughter thing. "Ms. Jill" was not what I expected that first day we arrived at her house. I was picturing one of those Summer Sanders, Olympic swimmer types—young, cocky, and jockish. Ms. Jill was an ordinary middle-aged woman, like the aunt you always looked forward to seeing at the family reunion. It didn't take long to notice she had the magic touch with children and easily gave Barney a run for his money.

Regularly toting my laptop along to satisfy my compulsiveness to work while Jessie practiced in Jill's backyard pool, one day Ms. Jill offered the poolside bonus room to escape the hot glaring sun. From the couch I could simply turn my head and watch Jessica work her backstroke. It was a blast watching them in action. Jessica would accomplish the simplest task, and Ms. Jill would cheer and carry on as if she had won a gold medal. At the end of each lesson, out came Jill's supply of Popsicles, oatmeal pies, and juice boxes. While Jessie enjoyed her treat, Jill and I would sit and chitchat while she waited for her next student to arrive. As the summer wore on, I began learning more bits and pieces about her.

Ms. Jill's lifework and passion was teaching severely handicapped children, which explained why half her swim students had severe disabilities. For the past seventeen years she had served in various roles working with special-needs children in the city's public school system. Sometimes while drying off Jessica and gathering up stuff before leaving, I observed her with these kids. She joyfully interacted with them, moving at their pace with the patience of someone focused on the person not the task. This amazed me, being one who gets nervous and awkward around handicapped children. One little girl, Molly, was autistic and frightened by water but benefited from aquatic muscle therapy. Her feet barely wet on the first stair into the pool, she began screaming and crying uncontrollably. Kneeling beside her, Ms. Jill wrapped loving arms around her until fear gave way to trust.

Again working inside one hot August day, nature called

and I ventured around the corner past her bookshelves in search of the facilities. You can catch the drift of folks by what they read, and on my way back, I couldn't help myself. Scanning titles, red flags immediately waved like banners at halftime of a college football game. In disbelief, I pulled a few books off the shelf, hoping for some explanation. *Please, no. Surely Ms. Jill isn't a li . . . li . . . li—no, she can't be—nice Ms. Jill? No, there's no way she can be . . . oh my gosh, she is—Ms. Jill is a liberal! Who else would read books by Al Franken or be interested in biographies of Bill Clinton? Come to think of it, she didn't seem to join in the day we all bashed the ludicrous idea of Hillary as president.*

The implications were staggering. First of all, Ms Jill *obviously* wasn't Christian. Apparently the sweet, compassionate swim-instructor gig was cover for the communist brainwashing of my daughter and others—all a part of some sinister master plan to seize power and corrupt America. Maybe that's why Jessica was now interested in insects and creepy-crawlers. Ms. Jill was probably sending her on secret assignments to locate some endangered spider so they could bulldoze my home and turn my property into a protected area. It was all starting to fall into place. Ms. Jill's travel outside the country likely related to the formation of a one-world government. Her field of education provided plenty of opportunities to conspire with those Harvard and Berkeley libs over green tea or during one of those sicko "art" exhibits.

No matter how hard I tried imagining Ms. Jill as one of those man-hating, election-rigging, Ten Commandments–banning, global-warming-alarming, tax-happy, freedom-assaulting, homosexual-marriage-promoting, Hollywood-adoring flaming liberals, I just couldn't quite make her peg fit in my preconceived hole. I needed to know: Was she or wasn't she one of *them*? It was time for covert operations of my own. If I kept bringing up controversial news stories, certainly she would tip her hand. No such luck. In frustration, I popped the big one to bait her. With a mouth full of oatmeal pie I said, "I wonder who will run for president next time."

She replied, "Who knows." Then she added, "Does it really matter?"

"What do you mean?" I asked.

"Well, Republican or Democrat, they're all so busy attacking each other, how do they accomplish anything outside of demonizing their opponents? I'd vote for any of them helping folks like the Ortiz family. They can't afford therapy for their daughter; that's why I only charge fifteen dollars per session. Whoever's president, either way, I'll just keep doing what I do."

Perhaps Ms. Jill's mini diatribe is nothing more than the naive and simplistic view of a public school teacher giving swim lessons on the side. Even so, her words had manufactured a shoe that sadly fit my foot too well. "Demonizing" her was comfortable, easy, and a boon to my self-esteem. Keeping up with my favorite political commentary blogs and often arranging my schedule to catch my beloved talk-radio shows, I was far more passionate about being Republican than being Christian, even confusing one with the other. Isn't the term "Christian Democrat" an oxymoron?

I began to see the meaninglessness of it all one afternoon in my front yard after passionately debating politics with a non-Christian neighbor. Getting all red in the face and almost in tears, she stormed off to her house, leaving me standing there with my "words of truth" still floating in the dialogue bubble above my head. Right or not, what did it really accomplish? She's now even more convinced that the other side is wacked-out and closed-minded, and I'm now excluded from her list of people with whom she can hash out the difficult questions of life. Something just didn't seem quite right when "them" now included my next-door neighbor and Ms. Jill, who had practically become my daughter's biggest fan and hero.

Maybe "us" and "them" is an illusionary tactic of the *real* enemy, and there is really no "them" but just one "us." Perhaps Christ desired to touch the lives of my neighbor and Jill through mine, but none of this was possible by making them political adversaries. Then why do I perpetuate that illusion— and what is it doing for me? Am I deriving value from being right politically, needing someone to be wrong? Does criticizing and blaming others serve to cover my own tracks of insult and injury in the world? Have I confused a war of words with rolling up my sleeves and actually doing something about all the issues and problems I claim to care about? Maybe demonizing people *out there* distracts me from the demons of pride and selfishness within myself. In the fourth chapter of his New Testament letter, James asks, "What causes fights and quarrels among you?" (v. 1 NIV). Answer: "They come about because you want your own way, and fight for it deep inside yourselves" (v. 1 MSG).

I'm wondering if set free from that struggle deep within for worth, purpose, significance, meaning, and love, I could see people more through God's eyes. Jesus said that God "sent me to announce pardon to prisoners and recovery of sight to the blind, to set the burdened and battered free." Maybe there's just *one* classification of people on planet Earth: imprisoned, empty, unfulfilled, broken people in need of the life only Christ can give.

Being "all of the above" and "none of the above" in a strange sort of way works for me. The "all of the above" part refuses to dismiss or shut down people just because they are not of my political persuasion, and recognizes we are all simultaneously pupils and professors, each person with something worthwhile to learn and teach. Sometimes the most unexpected people, like my six-year-old's swim instructor, contribute to our understanding of both the problems and the solutions. Politics hoodwinks us into thinking of one another as the enemy, but after you eliminate the crazies on all sides, don't most of us have a stake in many of the same issues? Don't we basically want similar things a government within reason can help provide? Does anyone really want unnecessary poverty, injustice, crime, or polluted water? We may disagree on how to get there, but do any of us want failing and unsafe schools for our kids? Maybe none of us really wants a total victory. After all, don't capitalists like parks, and don't environmentalists ride petroleum-based vehicles to get there?

The apostle Paul said once, "I have become all things to all [people] so that by all possible means I might save some" (1 Corinthinas 9:22 NIV). Wasn't Paul basically saying he could find enough common ground with anyone in order to press toward weightier matters? God has recently supplied an example of this in a rock musician icon. For a long time I had a hard time trying to figure out whether Bono of the Irish band U2 was a Democrat or a Republican. One minute he'd be hanging out with Clinton; the next day he'd be at the White House doing lunch with W. He has nice and not-so-nice things to say about both parties. Then I finally figured out that Bono's faith has compelled his ambition of alleviating AIDS, poverty, and hunger in the two-thirds world, and he will be both Democrat and Republican if necessary to do that.

The "none of the above" part remembers I am foremost a citizen of another kingdom altogether, and I am in the world to nurture, nourish, and evoke an alternative reality beyond anything summed up by any one political ideology. Maybe Jesus's life made plain the inadequacies of the world's power structures and put on display its failed claims to better our lives. Implicit in his announcement of a new kingdom are the failings of the present one. His prominent solidarity with marginal people demonstrated the new reality where the meek and helpless are conduits of his grace more so than the rich and powerful. Earthly affluence and clout do not compare to what Jesus gives, and only those with a humble heart will receive it. Having no recognized position or authority within the religious or political institutions of his day, this meager small-town carpenter's ways busted up political, religious, and economic corruption, melted gender and racial prejudice, and evoked compassion for the insignificant and disenfranchised. That's pretty good for someone who never held public office. Jesus said his followers are the salt and light of the world. Maybe the same courage of Martin Luther King Jr. and the same compassion of Mother Teresa are available to every believer through Christ living in us.

I can spend my time and energy arguing with Ms. Jill, or I can join her in our common concerns. As believers, we have the heart of Jesus inside, compelling us to seek solutions to the world's needs. The Spirit leads some into politics, and God often uses them to confront and correct the institutional and systemic realities that breed injustice and inequality. But doesn't God offer all of us ultimate hope that regardless of which political party wields power, he is present with us and satisfies our deepest need? God had his ways of busting up a few of my own red-state conservative prejudices, including a flamingly liberal swim teacher. Hillary as president or not, you can't stamp out the life of God and his kingdom. Ms. Jill was right. I'll just keep doing what I do, or rather, keep depending on Christ to do what he does in and through me.

I'm going to vote next November, but I don't think I'm going to stick a campaign sign in my front yard as in years past. I don't want to exasperate the neighbor who already won't even talk to me. I know we both seem to have a concern for the aged who live in our neighborhood, and we used to work together to check up on and do yard work for a couple of elderly widows nearby. I'm thinking it's a start in identifying something we both care about. I wonder if she likes U2?

twelve

Sex, Lies, and Paratroop Deployment (Rescued Varsha)

Worldview

FROM NASHVILLE, WE COVERED 8,792 MILES TO GET there, and soon after arriving I was plunged into an evil I hoped existed only in nightmares. I would have long since conveniently buried this experience beneath a mountain of rationalizations if I hadn't looked deep into the vacant eyes of a twelve-year-old sex slave and vowed never to forget. Her expression cannot be purged from memory, and sometimes my mind plays tricks by imposing her face on some little girl I see walking in the mall or playing at the park. Returning to my past world of ignorance would relieve my grief, but it's impossible to go back.

There are some details about my rude awakening in South Asia that I cannot tell you, including our specific locations. I traveled with a small band of highly trained professionals from International Justice Mission, which covertly deploys operatives around the globe to rescue victims of horrific human rights crimes, usually involving children. I saw *Batman Begins*, but I didn't realize there are actually people who risk their lives under cover of night, swooping in amid the horror to save innocent young lives from the clutches of evil. These people are real heroes, and I met them in the dark alleys of one of the largest red-light districts in the world.

Until then, my most courageous endeavor was scooping up a half-dead mouse our cat dragged up on the back deck, terrifying Pam and Jessica. A vaguely humorous scuffle ensued as things momentarily got ugly, but eventually the mission was accomplished. (Have you ever tried battling a mouse with a dustpan?) Not to say my Christian practices failed to embolden me. Hey, I can pass out church coffee mugs to strangers and do door-to-door neighborhood "surveys" with the best of them. I wasn't quite prepared, however, for these IJM guys answering the WWJD question by endangering their lives to free people most of the world wouldn't miss (in a nice kind of way, of course).

My job was to tag along, do exactly as I was told, and witness this heartbreaking tragedy with my own eyes. Arriving on an oppressively humid night, I taxied down into the red-light district with a guy I'll call Ron. I was briefed on the drive that we would work undercover, posing as customers looking for action to identify brothels forcing young girls into prostitution. Peeing in my pants became a distinct possibility, and that little form I'd signed about "going at my own risk" began taking on meaning I'd never imagined. I am a terrible liar and actor; how was I supposed to play a pervert looking to have sex with little girls?

Less than two minutes after our feet hit the pavement, a pimp approached and offered a tour of the prime spots in exchange for ten bucks. (Westerners get first-rate treatment because exchange rates exponentially increase their spending potential.) Ron did all the talking, plunging us into a sea of nightlife. An abrupt turn down a grungy narrow alley finally brought us to what looked like an abandoned old building.

We entered by climbing a steep stairway that dumped us out on a small landing outside a door that lacked an external knob. After a distinctive knock, the door opened into a dimly lit and glitzy lounge complete with plush 1970s-style carpeting on the floor and walls. Escorted to a comfy wraparound sofa, we sat next to real "customers" (mostly Americans), who could have easily passed for my dentist or the guy who coaches my daughter's soccer team. No one spoke. We just sat there staring at this elevated makeshift catwalk directly in front of us. Anger began seething within me, and I felt I could actually kill somebody without regret. After what seemed an eternity, the lights went off and the catwalk brightened. Soft music began playing as the back door swung open, and a line of scantily dressed little girls made up with mascara and high heels wobbled out to present themselves. I was reeling inside.

Images often associated with "escort services" and "men's clubs" where glamorous sexy goddesses summon John Doe to a night of orgasmic bliss are far from the aberration that was playing out just two feet in front of me. These ten- to fifteen-year-old girls looked pathetic and terrified as they were chided by the brothel owner to look energetic and maintain eye contact with customers who were making their rape selection. The younger they were, the more you paid. The littlest girls didn't come out. You had to specifically ask for them and show you had that kind of cash. Suddenly I was meeting the gaze of one little girl in a long black wig. Quickly glancing away, I noticed she continued staring right at me—or was it right through me? I wished for a cape and one of those superhero rescue gizmos to snatch her out of harm's way.

Those obscure headlines at the bottom of page D14 were now part of *my* world. Not wanting to remember or have anything to do with it doesn't work. The reality just won't go away or wash off. I've tried rationalizing, telling myself there are too many for me to make a difference, and it's those people and their governments who are to blame, and only they can fix it. I can't be responsible for people on the other side of the world and wouldn't know what to do in the first place. Besides, I have problems to address where I live (but I really don't). Certainly God's justice will eventually straighten all this out and everyone will get their just deserts. I tried all that mumbo jumbo and more.

But there I was, face-to-face with this horrified little girl staring at me, her shoulders so slight they couldn't keep the straps of her lingerie up. Despite all my sensible reasoning, it didn't add up to a very good answer to the WWJD question. Something from the well of my being cried out, "Do something!" It would be worth the effort, the reward far exceeding the cost. IJM had supplied the opportunity for me to be part of meeting the most obvious need of girls like this, the need to be set free. Posing as customers, we acted unimpressed with each lineup of girls shown us in order to be taken to several spots. This enabled us to document the particular brothels using minors, information that would later be used to organize a brothel raid and rescue operation. IJM was banking on my greatest contribution being made once I returned back home by raising awareness of the horrific plight of children forced into prostitution.

During the cab ride back, Ron detailed the terrifying trap that captured these girls. Lured to the city by the promise of earning money as domestic household servants, they are taken captive, transported by night to a brothel, and sold to the highest bidder. Locked in a room the size of a closet, they are told they will be providing sex to customers on demand. When the first customer comes, the child resists and fights back. The brothel owner beats her into submission with iron rods and electrical cords. She finally consents and begins providing sex six days a week, with up to ten customers daily. She is rationed one meal a day and not allowed to leave the brothel. When touring their "bedrooms" (four to six girls crammed together per dingy room) I almost lost it emotionally upon discovering that the same little girls forced to give sex still sleep with stuffed teddy bears and rabbits.

My worldview was turned upside down in the length of time it took to walk past the line of little girls waiting outside a clinic to receive treatment for AIDS and every sexually transmitted disease imaginable. I couldn't get back on the plane to Nashville quick enough.

I've done my share of globe-hopping, traveling to parts of the world most wouldn't be too interested to vacation in. One has a lot of time to kill on those long international flights, especially if you're like me and can't sleep well on planes. Flying home from South Asia, my books were stuffed in the bottom of my duffel bag, lost somewhere in the abyss of the overhead compartment. I decided I didn't want to risk waking up the kid next to me, who had finally stopped crying and gone to sleep. I had read every newspaper, was not interested in purchasing a thingamabob from the *Sky Mall* magazine, and had already seen *Father of the Bride* twice. So I sat and I thought. . . .

Have you ever stopped to wonder, *Where was God today?* Yes, I know God is "omnipresent," but I mean specifically, where was God today? Where did he go? What did he see? How did he feel? I began imagining God present at that miraculous moment a precious life was born into the world, the joy and marvel of the newborn bearing God's image and uniquely fashioned by his hands. Taking in the beauty of a brilliant blazing sun slowly descending behind endless ocean waves, I have felt the company of the Creator amid the splendor of his handiwork. Jogging a woodland trail one autumn morning I passed an aged couple leisurely strolling in conversation hand in hand. God must have been there smiling as these soul mates shared a ripe and tender love, a gift from God, who is himself named Love. These simple but magnificent miracles inspire love and adoration for God deep within and draw me to him.

Somewhere over the Atlantic, forty thousand feet above the earth, these nice thoughts about God gave way to disturbing images I wish I could forget from my trip. Now the question, where was God today? tortured me. Today a ten-year-old girl is being strapped down tight to a bed and brutally and repeatedly raped. God is present. Today an eight-year-old emaciated boy is covered with a cardboard box and left to die. Slowly he slips into unconsciousness. God is present. Today a young mom of three wails in bed as her skeletal body writhes with the unrelenting agony of AIDS. God is present. Still, I grew angry. Why was God pushing these horrors in my face? I was emotionally spent and wanted to go home to *my* world. God could have *that* world; that was his deal, he's God; I didn't live in *that* world.

Or did I?

Sitting in 13D, I uncovered something unsettling about myself. I don't really want a "relationship" with God. Here's what I want. I want to share with God all I feel, all I need, all that grieves me, all that makes me happy, the puzzling things, the fun things, and the hard things, but I would prefer that God keep his stuff to himself. I don't want to hear about his pain and share in his grief. I don't mind listening to God as long as I'm receiving solutions, answers, and advice. Maybe what I really want is a divine vending machine: pop in my prayer, press the button for my need, and I'm good to go. A professional live-in massage therapist and a Starbucks within walking distance would be nice too.

Any relationship involves two people, you and the other. It seems that in a "relationship" with God, we would desire to listen to the Other to learn what the Other is really like. But how is this possible without going through the adventure of each day with the Other? Can we personally and intimately know someone without sharing experiences, doing things together—little things as well as big things, and taking the risks of love together? Wouldn't we want to learn how to love those whom the Other loves, to see them through his eyes? We would want to rest and celebrate together, to share beautiful things, to laugh together. But wouldn't we also want to enter into the pain and grief the Other feels when pain, injustice, and cruelty are inflicted upon those he loves? In every abusive home where a child cries in fear and pain, and in every city street where a homeless person shivers under newspapers on the pavement, the living Christ is there. Whether it's across town or on the other side of the globe, suffering people surround us. Maybe "carrying Jesus's cross" is our free choice to become compassionately involved with him in the pain of others and be partners with God in bringing healing and transformation.

Just a small glimpse into God's world was enough for me. It's staggering to consider the intensity of anger and anguish I felt witnessing just a few injustices compared to what God must feel being personally and fully present to countless such heinous horrors 24/7. You'd have to be comatose not to feel God's hurt and anger ooze from the pages of Scripture over the oppression of the weak and vulnerable. Even after all my sophisticated exegesis of the Old Testament prophets and words of Jesus, I can't seem to get away from the fact that the main message of God to his people about injustice is to get off our rear ends and do something! This goes way deeper than feeling guilty about doing more; I'm trying to figure out how I got to the place where the things that break the heart of God are so marginal to mine.

I'm starting to wonder if I can even have a "relationship" with God this way, and I'm left with the question of how much I really want to know God. There's no having it both ways. Whether I like it or not, the God who dances over the breathtaking sunrise weeps over each victim of brutality.

Any relationship runs the risk of drifting apart over time. Take boy meets girl. In the hunting phase (or "dating" phase), guys become mysteriously and happily engaged in virtually everything the woman has interest in, including endless browsing at Pier 1 and watching Brad Pitt movies. We become brainwashed in love. College football, working out, and playing golf are easily sacrificed on the altar of love. They get married, and five years later, she's at the mall with a friend, and he's at home TiVo-ing the big game and watching *Terminator 5* while running on the treadmill. They have grown apart due to their separate interests. When I started off with Jesus, I wanted to know everything about him. I would have gone anywhere and done anything at any cost. As the years rolled on, somehow I became less interested in him and more interested in me. More specifically, what he could do *for* me. Rather than a relationship, my Christianity morphed into some sort of divine self-help philosophy, problem-solving plan, and life-improvement strategy.

The day before leaving we traveled far outside the city where I met a sixteen-year-old-girl named Varsha. After four years of being locked away and languishing in a brothel, one night a first-time paying customer behind closed doors strangely wanted something other than sex. Instead, this IJM operative asked the frightened little girl to trust him. She provided enough information for him to begin organizing a brothel raid. Several months later, under the cover of darkness, a twenty-four-passenger van slowly crept down the alley behind her brothel. Without warning, a surge of armed men kicked open the front door and seized the house in a fracas of commotion. The back door was swiftly secured, and Varsha and a line of other girls were rushed out amid gunfire into the waiting van. While the van squealed off into the night, the brothel owner and customers were subdued, cuffed, and hauled away. Mission accomplished.

These IJM guys have a slightly different picture of Jesus than most of us do, convinced that if he were bodily present, his boot would have been the first kicking in the door. Most churches try to soften up and tame these kinds; you know, make them more compassionate and caring. Maybe the kingdom of God needs a few more who are willing to kick some tail and take names if necessary. Sure, we need to pray for victims of injustice, but has anyone thought of, well, like, *rescuing* them? My afterlife view of justice is real convenient since neither I nor my daughter is the one being beaten senseless with electrical cords.

I had a few moments alone with Varsha on a bench in the outdoor courtyard of the recovery ranch where she now lives. We sat and talked. I learned that being saved from the brothel was just the first step on her long and difficult road to freedom. It was going to take a lifetime to recover from the physical, emotional, and spiritual damage she had experienced. She knows one thing: this Jesus must be worth knowing if his followers risk their lives to rescue nobodies like her. Reaching into a brown paper bag, she bashfully pulled out a braided leather necklace and presented it to me. She made it herself. Part of the healing process had been her discovering a talent for making jewelry and dresses, which she sold at the market.

It was time for her to go; she had an appointment at the AIDS clinic in the city and an afternoon counseling session. I felt awkward and didn't know what to say. Wanting to hug her, I had become timid myself. Time was ticking, and so I clumsily asked, "Do you mind if I give you a hug good-bye?" As we embraced, I close my eyes. This was a holy moment. In my arms was a precious and priceless daughter of God. One million new girls every year around the world are forced into child prostitution. Can someone like me or you really make any difference in such a massive sea of hurting people? It may not seem like much, but in moments like this, the ability to impact one life means a lot. God knows this one by name, and now she is free.

Sometimes what happens in our world is absolute evil, unimaginable chaos, and a stunning reversal of God's intent for creation. When my heart is broken open by suffering, especially suffering caused by human selfishness and cruelty, I meet a more complex God than I would prefer. Sometimes he is an *un*comforting God who does not provide easy, consoling answers to my pleading question, Why? At other times he is a *dis*comforting God, and his grief is simultaneously a cry for justice that enters creation like a mighty storm, rousing God's people from their sleep. While we wait in the darkness and ask God, "Why did you let this happen?" God hurls the question back to us: "Wake up, people, to what is happening. Why do *you* let this happen in the world I gave you?"

Whenever people are victims of injustice, God desires intervention. Some people in our world suffer from lack of food, water, shelter, or medical care. I'm beginning to see there's a whole other category of suffering in the world, namely, oppression. It's a crime of opportunity when powerful people exploit the weak and vulnerable by taking what they have or forcing them to do what they otherwise wouldn't. This grieves and angers God, and we reflect his image in us when we refuse to tolerate it. This God is both powerful and vulnerable in ways that are consistent with relationship and with life. He cares deeply about the well-being of every person in every community. He is passionate about wholeness and peace. He also hardwired humanity with free will. With that will, people commit injustice and believers ignore it. To live faithfully in relationship with God requires facing the whole truth of our world, looking honestly at our part in it, and being true to our identity as sons and daughters of God in the midst of it. This *dis*comforting God forces us to face reality and mobilizes us to do something about it.

Whether it's across the ocean or across town, it's never been about the *number* of people I can help relative to the size of the need. It's about relationship. With God. With one another. This one young girl in the middle of nowhere matters to him, and as we embrace, I feel she's starting to matter to me. We say our good-byes; she goes her way, and I go mine. Almost nine thousand miles is a long way to travel, but I think the distance between God and me is shrinking.

thirteen

The Great Reversal
(Father Jeff)

Religion

TO SAY I WAS RAISED CATHOLIC IS A STRETCH. TO BE MORE accurate, there was a string of years when as a youth I was made to attend Catholic Mass. Though I never doubted there was a God, my life was preoccupied with too many other things to be interested in the Almighty. Had I thought God could help me meet girls or pass algebra, I probably would have become an altar boy. As it turned out, I rarely dated, had to repeat a grade of high school, and never made it as far as confirmation.

My senior year of high school, the kicker on our football team, Chuck Young, took an interest in me. Every Friday morning before school we went to McDonald's for breakfast, and Chuck sometimes talked about his personal relationship with God. One evening as I was laid up in a hospital bed with a football injury, Chuck stopped by to see me. During our visit he asked if I'd be interested in knowing God for myself. Carrying a heap of hurt inside from years of abuse and clueless about the future direction of my life, I figured if God were half what Chuck described him to be, then I just might have a fighting chance. I said yes. My mother, brother, and I lived in a small apartment at the time. With mother passed

151

out on the front room couch and my brother watching porn movies in his bedroom, I could soon be found locked up in my room reading the Bible and talking to Jesus.

I guess it's possible I would still be a Catholic today if it weren't for the fact that the campus priest didn't take too kindly to my questions about discrepancies between certain points of Catholic theology and all the new things I was learning from reading the Bible. Looking back at it now, I was oblivious at the time to how threatening my questions were and I asked them, genuinely expecting some sufficient explanation. Instead, I ended up one day running into (almost literally, as I came close to mowing him down in the student center parking lot) the campus director of Campus Crusade for Christ. We hit it off. That coincidental meeting set the stage for a twenty-year journey through Protestantism, which included a seminary degree and years in the pastorate.

My two-decade evangelical odyssey bred prejudicial feelings toward Catholics as I was told they believed in salvation by works, worshipped Mary, and ascribed godlike status to human leaders such as priests and the pope. It was clear from my church history class that Catholics had made a real mess of things, and the Protestant Reformation got Christianity headed back in the right direction. (Of course, later I realized that we evangelicals were guilty of our own indiscretions of peddling "grace, but . . ." theology, gushing over prominent evangelicals in politics, music, and megaministries, and depending on preachers as the pipeline of truth.) I even lumped all those "collar-wearing" denominations together—Catholics, Episcopalians, Anglicans, Orthodox; they were all the same to me. Of course, my false notions only served to tee me up for a good humbling.

Beginning with my trip to visit Kit in Connecticut, I became increasingly exposed to Catholic Christians, starting with several books that Kit recommended by the likes of Thomas Merton, Thomas Keating, and Henri Nouwen. Through my reading, I began recognizing that there were several aspects to knowing God I had missed in my evangelicalism. In fact, after leaving the pastorate and settling into the rank and file of churchgoers, I grew increasingly disillusioned with my church involvement, which didn't seem to be getting me any closer to God. The conclusion I came to at the time was that any form of organized or institutional church (Catholic, Baptist, non-denominational, whatever) must be flawed, and perhaps God never intended people to relate to him through services, programs, and meetings. Maybe "church" had devolved into a man-made bureaucracy seeking to control and manage God.

Eventually Pam and I left organized church, and coming upon a few others on similar journeys, we began hanging out and connecting our lives. We all discussed the concern of how to help and encourage our kids in their relationship with God now that there was no longer any children's program to send them to. Though we knew they mostly needed to see and experience it lived out in the ebb and flow of daily life, we were also led to provide opportunities for them to freely explore, experience, and enjoy God together as kids. This all led to our starting a Good Shepherd atrium on the Williamses' farm. As time went on, more families joined our group. Indoor space became an issue, and we began brainstorming possibilities. Coffee almost came spewing out of my mouth when someone suggested checking into using a room at the little Episcopal church down the street. Are you kidding? The whole point was trying to get away from institutional church. I made no comment about the Episcopal church option, but we all agreed to follow up on any promising leads. Days turned into weeks, then months. Driving here and there (sometimes passing the Episcopal church) searching for a suitable place proved fruitless. The group finally decided to contact the church and arrange a meeting with Father Jeff. Anticipating our meeting, I could not see how I was going to explain a group of burned-out Baptists wanting to use his Episcopal facilities on a regular basis . . . at no cost. "No, we don't want to become Episcopalian. We just want to use a couple of your rooms for free."

We arrived at the church before Father Jeff. When he pulled up in his black Toyota Tundra, I was a little surprised. Priests drive trucks? When Father Jeff hopped out of the truck, I noticed he was wearing a pair of jeans. Priests go casual? Entering his office, Father Jeff insisted on everyone having a round of cold drinks, and we all took seats around a table. Having had a phone conversation with Joanna Williams prior to our meeting, Father Jeff was aware of our need for space, yet there were lots of details needing to be addressed. Being the fearless, gutsy, assertive leader I am . . . I waited for Joanna to initiate the conversation.

Bracing myself for a theological battle of epic proportions, out of the blue Father Jeff launched into a diatribe about the "kingdom of God." To him, there was only one Jesus, who graciously and indiscriminately extended his life and love to anyone willing to receive it. As far as Father Jeff was concerned, denominational affiliation made no difference, and we were all sons and daughters of God in Christ, making us brothers and sisters on earth. Father Jeff insisted, "Whatever is ours is yours, including use of our facility." I thought, *Dorothy, this isn't Kansas. I must be dreaming. Did I just hear a priest refer to a Baptist as his brother in Jesus and offer a blank check to use his parish facilities?*

With time I discovered that Father Jeff's views were not that mushy-gushy ecumenical stuff where what you believe doesn't matter. This was different. Father Jeff was big on the Bible and held a short nonnegotiable list of beliefs any evangelical would agree with, but he didn't feel the need to convert everybody into Episcopalians. The Episcopal way and tradition were deeply meaningful to him, but he believed God was big enough to meet folks where they were and walk with them on whatever road they chose. To Father Jeff, the kingdom of God was rich and beautiful, partly because it was so diverse.

This was all too good to be true, and I kept my eyes wide open as Father Jeff and I got to know each other. I was waiting for the shoe to fall when he would tie me down to douse me in holy water. We began meeting every now and then at a nearby coffeehouse where I mustered enough nerve to inquire about all the senseless things I thought Episcopal types did. For example, it grated on me to see him in public places wearing his sanctified garb. Why the collar? Isn't it basically an ego trip? Hey everyone, look at me; I'm special, I'm worthy, I'm the God expert and you're not. My Christianity was more than a fashion statement, and my identity wasn't based on some overstarched claim to spiritual superiority.

Father Jeff explained that his collar marked him as a "fool" in the eyes of the world. There was no hiding his association with Jesus. To him, Christianity was not just adding a little fish to the rear bumper of one's business-as-usual life but placing God in the center and building out from there, even if it looked moronic and worthless to everyone else. The collar was symbolic of his daily worship, "presenting his body as a living sacrifice" amid snickers and sneers. Come to think of it, I enjoyed the convenience of turning on or off my association with Jesus when it suited me. I could get irritated with my waitress or grocery store cashier and they'd never be the wiser. Sure, I was all for being a "fool" for Christ, as long as I could control just what kind of fool I was going to be—you know, like a trendy fool who's into spirituality and social activism.

I decided to attend one of Father Jeff's smells-and-bells services. On the way in, the first person I noticed was a young bald guy with earrings in both ears. He was wearing a short-sleeved T-shirt, and tattoos of dragons and serpents covered both arms. My first thought was, *Shouldn't this guy be at the cool church down the street? What's he doing at this high-brow gig?* Remembering now, I picture myself as the prover-bial deer caught in the headlights as the service started. Every element caught me off guard: all the sitting, standing, kneel-ing, reciting, praying, and singing. I managed to mess up the whole "passing the peace" part too. This older woman took my hands, and looking into my eyes said, "The peace of Christ to you." I responded with some idiotic comment about what a beautiful autumn day it was.

Though I'm not sure I quite got it, a few things about the experience stuck with me. I was used to contemporary church services rolling out a big techno stage production of upbeat Christian music, drama, and relevant sermons projected on screens with all kinds of cool graphics. Everything culmi-nated with the charismatic leader delivering his dynamic, entertaining, life-changing message.

Father Jeff's deal was refreshingly unlike this. The center-piece of the whole service was the Eucharist, encountering the risen Christ and receiving his life anew through the elements of bread and wine. Everything built up to and revolved around Christ—his life, his death, his resurrection. People even stood and paid special homage when the words of Jesus were read aloud. Father Jeff's sermon wasn't more than ten minutes. It was clear the attraction here was not Jeff, but Jesus. Though I was the inerrancy-defending, card-carrying evangelical, there was more Scripture and Jesus in this service than in six months of the typical evangelical fare. Maybe Father Jeff didn't need to say much. Perhaps the medium was the message. The root word of "Christianity" is *Christ*. There is no life apart from him. Like his service, Christ is the axis around which everything revolves.

Over all the years I've attended Sunday church services, despite the feel-good reward of checking my attend-church box, corporate worship gatherings have been a struggle for me. During the praise music, I've sometimes stood and sung along with everyone else but failed to experience significant connection with God, feeling as though I was just going through the motions. This was troubling since so much emphasis was placed on these corporate worship gatherings. The subtle message seemed to be that getting worked up into visible emotion was a sure sign of "worship." I would look around and see others with rapturous expressions on their faces or raised hands, and wonder what was wrong with me. Jesus once said, "That's the kind of people the Father is out looking for: those who are simply and honestly *themselves* before him in their worship" (John 4:23 MSG, emphasis added). Some Sundays, honest worship for me would have simply been the quiet inner confession of trust that God was bigger than the hurt I was experiencing in life at the time.

Maybe predetermining and performing a set of songs to sing as "worship" isn't the only way. I often wonder what it would be like for people to simply circle around and offer their "worship" to God (prepared or spontaneously) however they choose. Perhaps a story shared of how Christ's life is producing wholeness, or a song, poem, or painting created

157

and offered in exaltation of the beauty, goodness, or justice of God. Maybe a passage of Scripture or ancient prayer read and mulled over in silence, or a time of listening and responding to the promptings of the Spirit. Reading a journal entry of personal conversation with God, or expressing one's heart to God through dance or music.

The teaching times in these contemporary praise services were often equally troubling. No matter how it was packaged on the screen, the bottom line normally seemed to be, here's what you need to do to be a good Christian and live a blessed life. In my own reading of the Scriptures, I came across all kinds of provocative teachings of Jesus about the kingdom of God, inner freedom and peace, and the mystery of his indwelling me, but these themes didn't seem to come up much in church.

Sitting in Father Jeff's service, God appeared to be reaching out to me through the simple reading of Jesus's words and commemoration of his death and resurrection. It was like the gospel was unfolding anew before my eyes and God was inviting me once again to rest in his forgiveness and depend on the life of the risen Christ within, evoking a sense of wonder and gratitude for all he has done for me.

I was beginning to see that it's not so much what one does but why one does it. Catholic Mass or Pentecostal praise-a-thon, High Church or home church, a person's motivation can be love and gratitude or fear and guilt. To be honest, I don't completely get some of the stuff Father Jeff is into and sometimes wonder if he thinks I'm a little "out there" myself, but maybe, just maybe, that's okay. We both desire to know Christ more intimately, love him more deeply, and follow him more courageously. The vision of the kingdom of God has taken hold of us both. Why do I care if he wants to swing some incense around and ring chimes? If he doesn't make me pray with rosary beads, I won't make him worship with my Switchfoot CDs.

To my surprise, a few weeks later Father Jeff invited me to speak at his service. I had hoped one of those bishop guys with the big hats wouldn't catch wind of this. The next Sunday morning Father Jeff gave me the nod, and I stood and walked down the aisle to the front of the altar. It was a slow walk; I wasn't used to wearing a robe and would rather not have tumbled before the crowd of congregants. When I arrived at my designated spot, I turned to face the group and spotted the guy with tattoos in the back left pew. Just down the hill our children were painting pictures, planting mustard seeds, and singing songs in rooms Father Jeff had let us convert into our special kids' place. One of those rooms was his office, which he had moved out of so we could use it. It wasn't just our kids; Father Jeff had asked if the few young children in his parish could join us. Why not?

Standing there, the comical irony of it all hit me. Father Jeff (an Episcopal priest) had just introduced me (an AWOL Baptist) as a "good friend and answer to prayer" who would be bringing the teaching for that Sunday's service. Somewhere God was laughing. The Gospel reading and my teaching text for that Sunday was Jesus's parable of the workers in the vineyard, which Jesus sums up with the words "So the last will be first, and the first will be last" (Matthew 20:16 NIV). I told the congregation that grace prevails in the kingdom of God, and strangely some people who seem to be the least deserving end up at the head of the line. There is something disturbing and scandalous about this. Are there no clear-cut rules to the kingdom of God? Don't we need to know who's in and who's out, who's right and who's wrong? Certainly we all can't be equally entitled to the favor of God? Would that be fair?

Father Jeff and I do not quite act or talk or think alike, or even believe all the same things, but we both know we are hopeless apart from God's grace, and we believe receiving what Jesus wants to give is the key. I wonder if Christianity seems so divided, not so much because there are varieties of Christian communities and denominations, but because we make these mutually exclusive claims to our group being the only (or best) representation of the Christian faith. Maybe differences of opinion that are honestly held can lead to profitable and fruitful discussion out of which a fuller comprehension of the truth may emerge. Since no church has a final and unambiguous grasp of divine truth, the true church of Jesus Christ can never be fully represented by any single one—Catholic, Episcopal, Baptist, Methodist, Presbyterian, Lutheran, Pentecostal, non-denominational, or emergent. Maybe we all are a little right and a little wrong and can get closer to the truth only by coming together. Getting to know Father Jeff helped me discover several vital things I was missing.

It saddens me how quick I am to criticize others. I remember back when I was so critical of Catholics, how I poked fun at the pope. But if half of what I later read and heard about Pope John Paul II was true, I can now understand why young people grieved openly in the streets at his death. Sick and tired of trendy Christianity and being shrink-wrapped in the latest church marketing label ("busters," "Gen Xers," "post-modernists," etc.), these kids saw in Pope John Paul II someone who represented a transcendent yet grounded spirituality. He demonstrated to these youth the deep compassion of Christ but didn't mince words concerning all the crap in the world, a compelling combination absent in many of their politicians and preachers. Maybe Generation X doesn't need the latest and greatest high-tech church service to attend but instead needs to see a few more holy fools, people whose lives revolve around the radical, foolish gospel.

We are all teachers and all students at the same time, and our understanding of the truth is contained in the community of believers spanning centuries, continents, traditions, and styles. Maybe I'm not the one guy who has miraculously and finally stumbled upon "it." Perhaps the Spirit has enlightened one or two others on some things I have missed. I'm such a dope . . . maybe some day these trees will thin out and I'll be able to see the forest.

Just days after I completed this chapter, Father Jeff resigned as priest of his Episcopal church and shared his desire to continue in ministry as a Catholic priest. He further explained he was planning to start a Catholic home church. I didn't think that was possible, but Father Jeff explained that the tradition of the church doesn't require buildings and bureaucracy to carry on. We think more alike than I thought. Maybe we should team up. Perhaps we will. I used to think that the deciding factor in knowing God was one's form of worship style or church life: traditional church versus contemporary church, seeker-targeted versus purpose-driven, high church versus home church, modern church versus postmodern church, institutional versus organic. After coming full circle to a greater appreciation for my Catholic roots, I realize now I was barking up the wrong tree by focusing on form and style. There will never be any wineskin capable of fully containing the life of God, but it's funny how criticizing everyone else's wineskin seems to distract a person from the life of God altogether.

After completing and reading this chapter, I've had to take

a step back. Have I grown critical of all forms of institutional or contemporary evangelical churches—swapping one form of prejudice for another? Thank God for Father Jeff. I think he'll help keep me straight.

....

fourteen

Left Behind
(Dominique, the Abandoned Boy)

....

Scars

NINE-YEAR-OLD DOMINIQUE LIVED IN PUBLIC HOUSING ON the east side of the city with his crack-addict mother. He has never met his father. A year ago, his older brother was shot and killed right before his eyes. Dominique loves his mother, and she was all he had, but in desperation she bartered temporary escape from life's tribulations through the cruel slavery of addiction. One Monday, Dominique's mother arranged to drop him off with a babysitter for the morning. Monday turned into Tuesday and then Wednesday. She never returned to pick him up. She was never going to come back. Of course Dominique didn't yet know all this. Though never having met, it was my fate to tell him.

As executive director of an inner-city organization for at-risk youth, I oversaw our group home for abused and abandoned boys. On Wednesday, I received a call from Doug and Kelly, the house parents of our group home. They explained receiving a young boy named Dominique earlier that morning. Since arriving, he had lain on his bed, completely unresponsive. It's a difficult adjustment for every boy, given the horrific circumstances each comes from. For example, Scott's father was in prison and his mom died from cancer. Then there are brothers Eric and Russell, whose prostitute mother's latest live-in boyfriend regularly beat them. Mitchell and his mom lived in hotel rooms shared by nieces, nephews, and whoever happened to wander in, including some older men who sexually abused Mitchell. Doug and Kelly were well acquainted with kids scarred by abuse, but their new arrival concerned them. I sensed it in their voices; something to them seemed very wrong with Dominique.

They called for two reasons. Being the director, if something is truly wrong, I need to help determine our course of action. Their main reason, though, was that they knew my childhood background and hoped I could reach out through my pain into Dominique's. Jumping in the car, I headed over to the group home. When I rolled in, all the guys were in the kitchen making lunch; well, I'm not sure Doug and Kelly would call it that, but they were enjoying themselves anyway. Little Eric ran over, wanting me to hoist him high over my head like I was about to give him a WWF-style body slam, my normal greeting for him. I obliged. Scott and I did a little give-and-take over his Cowboys and my Titans, ending in my chiding him once again for losing our last one-on-one game of basketball. After grabbing a few chips off someone's unwatched plate, I headed upstairs in search of Doug and Kelly.

I found them in the front room, and Kelly was distraught. She's such a softhearted girl, I've often worried if she would make it walled in by such catastrophic misery and heartache. She and Doug considered the boys brothers to their own two sons. After hearing the recap of Dominique's past few hours, I climbed the stairs to the bedrooms. I peeked inside the partly opened door. Dominique was sitting on the side of his bed, staring into space. Sadness began simmering within; I knew that look and its lonely paralyzing place of deadness. Memories took me back in time to opening the front door of apartment U-1 and being greeted by the sight of my mother sprawled unconscious on the couch. Dropping my schoolbooks, I had run over and shook her hysterically. Either she passed out from drinking or made good on her suicide threats to overdose on sleeping pills. Each time, it posed a cruel dilemma. Was I to call 911? But she would've been be furious if others had seen her like that. Eventually, just like Dominique, I, too, sat on the edge of my bed and drifted into oblivion.

Taking a seat on the bed next to him, he stares straight ahead without saying a word. We sit together in the silence. I hate this. I know that Dominique, like all the boys, doesn't have a chance of surviving if he doesn't get to the place of forgiveness. Few of them do. Through the last three years of working with abused and abandoned kids, I have learned their greatest obstacle in reaching wholeness is the black hole of bitter resentment. Perhaps it is their right to hate the people who beat, raped, neglected, and deserted them, but a bitter adulthood is no consolation for a stolen childhood. I have seen too many follow resentment behind bars and into caskets.

Jesus said, "Love your enemies," but what if your own flesh-and-blood father or mother locked you up all day in a tiny hall closet or failed to protect you from a sexual predator inside your own home? Despite my educational and pastoral background, I'm still utterly lost for words sitting beside Dominique on the bed. An imaginary conversation begins playing in my mind. *"Dominique, God loves you and wants to help you." "Yeah, right. Where was God when my brother was shot right before my very eyes? Where was God all those nights when I was at home, alone and afraid, while Mom was who knows where strung out on crack? Where was God when . . ."*

"Dominique, we care about you and are here to walk through all this with you." "Who are you? *I don't want you, and I don't want to be here! I want my mom! Where is she? Go find her. Bring her back!"*

As the agonizing silence lingers, I place my arm around his shoulder. It's a risk, but right now he is fearful and confused, trusting no one. To him, maybe we are the ones responsible for keeping him from his mom, or, worse yet, maybe it is us who took her away. He doesn't know me. I'm just some white man in a suit who doesn't know jack about his life or world. But he doesn't know that I've been there. I know he's hemorrhaging inside and needs another human being to give him permission and a safe place to hurt. He's held it together well up to now, but as Ecclesiastes 3 says, "There is a time for everything," and it was his "time to weep," at least for now.

With my arm around his shoulder, I say something like, "Well . . . this just stinks, doesn't it?" Staring straight ahead, Dominique eventually replies, "Yep." A drop of sadness rolls slowly down his face. He doesn't realize it, but even after all these years, something deep inside me is still weeping. Burying his face in his hands, the drops become streams as I sit beside him now with my own trickle of tears, half hurting over his loss, half aching over mine. We are both in pain, different maybe, but equally suffering. He's young and has hope that perhaps somehow things can magically be put back together. I have no such hope and ache over suffering's permanence. So my mind begins wandering through memories of my own journey.

I was well into my adulthood before squarely facing the scars of my childhood. I can even remember thinking to myself once how intact I seemed to be, given my traumatic upbringing. My bubble of blissful denial was popped when my marriage ended in divorce and I left the pastorate. Having been married in college and entering the ministry soon after, my adult identity revolved around the roles of husband and pastor. I felt a sense of security in the fact that I was doing what most normal people seemingly did: get a degree, identify a vocation, buy a house, open an IRA, and go on vacations. My sense of worth was sufficiency propped up by the steady praise I received from church members and peers for being a great speaker and leader.

When it all came crashing down, there wasn't anyone for me to call or turn to for help. Most normal people in the throes of calamity and heartache reach out to the people closest to them—perhaps a mother, father, sister, or brother. Not me. Calling them would have been like stopping a complete stranger on the street. Night after night, I lay awake in the dark, stalked by a cruel loneliness that refused to let me sleep. No matter how hard I tried, I couldn't imagine a scenario where a life worth living could emerge from the mess mine had now become. Stripped of my marital and ministry status, there were essentially only two remaining factors that defined who Jim Palmer was. The first was my name, which tied me to a biological family that for so many years had been my greatest source of pain. The second was my faith, which tied me to a spiritual family and a heavenly Father who loved me. Somehow I had managed to keep these two things separate, but time after time God kept informing me that he wanted those two parts of my life brought together. He wanted me to quit running from the hurts of my past and instead dive right into them.

One such instance occurred one day when I opened my Bible to Psalm 23, desperate for those "green pastures" and "quiet waters." A set of events began playing out vividly in my imagination, with Jesus wanting to take me somewhere. Jesus first passes by me as if not seeing me, but then he stops and slowly turns around, his eyes gazing deep into my weary soul. His expression invites me to follow. I do. At the top of a hill, I fall speechless (my wife and friends believe this to be a miracle for sure). Side by side with Jesus, I look out upon wide-open spaces filled with lush meadows and gently flowing streams. I close my eyes, slowly filling my lungs with pure air and smiling in response to a soft cool breeze fanning my face. Jesus cares for my soul. I'm at rest there next to him. I could stay with him on that bluff forever.

Jesus motions; he has some place farther he wants to take me. Why? I don't want to leave. Yet I want to be with Jesus, so I keep following. We walk along, and the air grows cold as dusk begins to claim the once blue skies. The trek becomes strenuous as we move along rocky paths in the dark shadows of towering boulders. Up ahead I see some sort of outdoor pavilion or shelter. Finally, a place to rest! I'm tired and hungry. As we approach the shelter, it appears there are tables and people seated around them. Jesus says nothing, but apparently we are having dinner with his friends.

Now close enough to make out the faces, I stop dead in my tracks, reeling. No, it can't be! It's them! Sitting there are my father, mother, and brother. Is this some sort of cruel joke? I trusted you, Jesus. I hate them! Why have you brought me here? Why are they here? I won't go! I turn to run, but I trip, falling hard upon the rocky trail. Lying in a heap, I realize there's nowhere to go. Ominous dialogue begins bouncing off the soaring boulders. I hear the voice of my sister screaming. My brother has erupted into another fit of rage and is beating my sister senseless in the backyard. I'm kicking him, but I can't get him off her. She's limp like a rag doll. He threatens that I'm next. I take off running and hide inside the house. He's done with her, and now he's after me. Shaking in fear, I huddle under blankets in the closet. "Please God. Please God. Please God. Please God."

My swirling mind shifts with another fearfully familiar voice. I'm awakened again in the middle of the night by my mother's sobs and screams. I don't know why she wants to kill herself. I try my best to make her happy. Why am I not enough? I hate myself! I am stupid and ugly and worthless! Isn't that why my father left, why he never calls, why he doesn't care about me?

My throbbing leg as I lie on the ground jolts me back to reality. Jesus stands before me offering his hand. I must be stupid. I'm going to take it. Then again, what else can I do? I arise and shake off the dirt. I am standing peacefully atop the hill next to Jesus in the gentle breeze. Maybe I *can* trust Jesus. As if knowing my thoughts, his eyes reply, *You can.* So I take his hand as he continues to lead me toward the pavilion. Darkness overtakes my soul with each step. It is unbearable and feels as though I am marching to my death.

Jesus walks me to the table of my enemies—father, mother, and brother. Seating me directly across from them, he sits down beside me. They have not spoken and perhaps are not permitted to speak. It's been so long, and looking them each square in the face unleashes a torrent of emotion—malicious anger, bitter hate, then an ache of sadness so deep and over-powering I hang my head. I feel nauseated. I want to die. Jesus turns to me; he knows my inner turmoil and assures me I am safe. With a gentle hand, he lifts my head, bringing my eyes to look deeply upon those on the other side of the table.

Right before my eyes, Jesus unmasks the powerlessness of those before me. Each of these family members is a source of such intense hurt. I can no longer fight back the tears. Not to worry; his nail-scarred hands reach up and wipe them from my face. No words are spoken as his loving presence touches places of deep sadness inside me. Love opens the eyes of my heart, and for the first time I see in Jesus's face a God who knows and shares my hurt. Standing me up, he places those nail-scarred hands firmly on my shoulders. With accepting eyes and a fierce love, he speaks mysterious words to me, or was it *for* me or maybe *into* me? I'm not sure. "Father, this one I have been given. By my stripes he is healed. May he walk in peace."

Across the table from my enemies, Jesus does something I have never been able to do for myself—overcome them. I feel liberated. Not from my hurt, but from its power to control and imprison me. Jesus announces that I am free to leave the table whenever I choose, leaving the ball and chain of resentment behind. Breaking the silence, I say, "Yes, Lord, it's time. I'm ready. Yes, Lord, I want to be free." Rising to my feet, I experience the lightness of a hiker dropping a heavy pack at the end of a long journey through the wilderness.

A few steps away, something inside compels me to turn back. I can't believe my eyes! No longer afraid of them, I feel sadness for them. There sits Mother with all her own hurts, the daughter of an alcoholic father who died when she was young. Heartbroken by the death of her first child, she would later become a single mom struggling to raise four kids without a husband. And Father, working two jobs and barely keeping his head above water, all the dreams he had to give up along the way, and all the hurts he carried and buried amid the chaos of it all. There's brother, abandoned, then adopted, but still lost, lonely, and angry inside. For the first time in my life, I was seeing these people who wounded me as wounded people themselves. Was it that they *didn't* love me or *couldn't*?

Looking over at Jesus, I ask, "What do I do?" He replies, "Let them go. Release them." There's a part of me that doesn't want to. I want to hate them. They hurt me and deserve my punishment and resentment for all the pain they caused me. I want to blame them. In some twisted way, it makes me feel good. I need it. I want to hate them. Jesus speaks again. "Jim, let them go!" Then it dawns on me, I can never truly walk in freedom unless I do. Jesus has forgiven them; so must I. Jesus wants us all free. He cares for my soul and theirs. Inside I feel my human weakness being trumped by the power of Christ emanating within me. I say, "Yes, Lord." I turn back to them. "Mom . . . Dad . . . brother, as Christ forgives you, so do I. You, too, go in the forgiveness and peace he provides."

Sitting on the bed next to Dominique that day was the start of a friendship that slowly grew in the days, weeks, and months that followed. Somewhere along the way, Dominique crossed that line of knowing he could trust me. It is one of the miracles our eyes are opened to, that our pain is not wasted. The healing and transformation Jesus had brought to my wounds was now becoming a source of Christ's life for Dominique. One day Dominique and I were shooting hoops in the driveway behind the group home. The hurt of being left behind was especially tormenting Dominique that day, and seeking relief, he asked, "What do I do?" I held the basketball in my arms, and what came to mind to say was, "Dominique, you must do the thing you know you cannot do."

Making no sense to Dominique, he gave me one of those "come again" looks. I went on to share with him how I had eventually come to this place in my own life of knowing that I could never truly overcome the wounds of my past without squarely facing them, and how for so many years I feared going to those places of deep hurt until I discovered that Jesus always went with me and it was safe. I knew it didn't all make sense to Dominique right then, but I prayed that our little chat would be a seed God would use in days ahead. Like me, Dominique will come to a point of desperation when he will long to be free. When he gets there, he will find the road to freedom requiring things of him he simply will not be capable of doing on his own. It is then, I pray, that he remembers our conversation and sees Jesus standing there with outstretched hands.

There are plenty of things *I* can do, but I'm starting to see that the life Jesus wants for me is beyond what I can manage on my own. There's a reason we shy away from and bury deep those things we know are not quite right. They scare us because we know how inadequate we truly are in the face of them. It's both easier and more difficult to live in a world we control, even if it's only an illusion. Maybe the way to "green pastures" and "quiet waters" passes through the "valley of the shadow of death."

Can you see Jesus on the edge of the Grand Canyon with one of those burros loaded down with rafts, tents, food, and supplies, saying, "Follow me to the other side, the kingdom of God?" Maybe Jesus's side job is being a wilderness adventure guide. Can you imagine him in the midst of some level-five rapids, saying, "Consider it pure joy, my brothers, whenever you face trials of many kinds"? Maybe I need a few more moments sitting next to Dominique. Trusting Jesus to lead us through our valleys, he begins to do within and through us what we could never do on our own. It's a rocky journey for sure, but we become stronger and freer as we depend on Christ's Spirit to guide us toward a way of living that is liberated from the power of life's hurts and sorrows. Upon reaching that summit, we will see all the things he planned for us—joy inexpressible, peace unimaginable, and love for the unlovable.

I'm seeing it now, and I'm dancing and laughing. I see it!

fifteen

Where the Rubber Meets the Road (Rick, the Tire Salesman)

Overflow

DESPITE ALL THE DENOMINATIONAL DISTINCTIONS I'VE COME across along the way, for the life of me, I cannot find any other litmus test Jesus insisted upon to authenticate his followers except love. This was unsettling when I realized that despite knowing Greek and Hebrew and the boxes in my attic filled with hundreds of my sermons on tape telling others how to be a Christian, I wasn't very loving. Winston Churchill cautioned, "However beautiful the strategy, you should occasionally look at the results." My version of Christianity wasn't making me much like Jesus.

Sure, I was nice . . . very nice. No, I was very, very nice and did a lot of very nice things. But nice isn't necessarily "love." You can run an inner-city organization caring for abused and abandoned children, start and lead a seeker-targeted and emergent church, and travel across the country speaking out on behalf of oppressed peoples around the world but still not necessarily love. You could feasibly do all of this merely to get God to like you, to feel good about yourself, or to distinguish yourself as a somebody. I had no problem being the guy to give the cup of cold water, but I wanted to be sure someone either saw it or heard about it, even if it was just a sermon illustration, you know—to encourage others. The simple math of this disturbed me; how many nice things would I be doing if there were no possibility of any other person on the planet ever finding out? Hmmm.

The person God has been using to teach me about love during this stretch of my life is a tire salesman. He never intended to teach me about love (or anything else). I've just learned by hanging out with him. Rick has no Bible degree, never served in any sort of vocational ministry, and does not attend any local "church." He likes a good cigar (Macanudos preferred, Rick adds), has a beer every now and then, and you often find him on the lake in his boat. But by far Rick's greatest passion in life is knowing God (not just knowing about God, but actually knowing God personally and intimately). His life is an example of an ordinary guy depending on Christ. I'm familiar with Christians who talk a good game but don't live it. I'm familiar with Christians who talk a good game and play at it enough to project and protect their image. I'm familiar with Christians who talk a good game and are paid and expected to live it. What I'm not as familiar with are people who just live it. Believe it or not, there are actually people like this. Like Rick.

One night we were drinking Kona (Hawaiian coffee for you non–coffee fanatics) at the Paradise coffee shop, shooting the breeze with Bob, who owns the joint. For a guy who runs a little café, Bob has insider information on all matters of importance. I could read the paper, watch the news, listen to NPR, or surf news blogs, but why? Bob can fill me in. Just about closing time, a ragged man ventured inside the rather small confines of Bob's lounge. He was a short, scruffy, pot-bellied chap with a coarse face, stumpy hands, and threads of blond hair hanging out from under his worn baseball cap.

Bob was busy behind the counter going through his end-of-day routine, with only Rick and I remaining . . . and now, the man. I was okay with orchestrating a strategic exit to avoid direct contact with the guy, but instead Rick greeted him and the guy pulled up a chair at the table next to ours. It is a commendable (even hip) thing to give money to programs and organizations that help the homeless, or perhaps serve as a volunteer dishing up Thanksgiving dinner, but you should never actually get personally involved with these people. Encountering them along the side of the road or in the supermarket parking lot, you might direct them to the local mission and perhaps even arrange a taxi ride if you are looking to go the extra mile. But you should never give them money or let them in your car or home, because they will probably kill you or blow all your dough on alcohol and drugs. I guess you could actually get to know one of them, but why? They're homeless people. You *help* homeless people; you don't get to know them.

These are some of the unspoken assumptions I learned along the way to becoming a good Christian. I didn't include the ones that justify doing nothing on the basis that such people are responsible for their own demise and that God helps those who help themselves. Right?

Evidently Rick didn't get the e-mail about never talking to the homeless, because without missing a beat, he grabbed John some coffee and settled into conversation with this broken-looking man as if he were his long-lost uncle. Whatever else he might need or ask for, it was clear to Rick that any person weary of traveling, with more miles still ahead, could use some java on a cold winter's night. Rick listened to his story, asking questions as if he really was interested, because strangely enough, he *was* really interested. Something within

Rick wanted to know this guy and was looking for some reason or way to help him. I've experienced other situations where someone, approached by a homeless person, began quizzing him like a prosecuting attorney searching for a contradiction in a suspect's alibi. Rick's chat with John was more like campfire conversation, where each person has a story worth telling and hearing. This was the first time in my life I had ever listened to a homeless person tell his story.

I've never had my head split open by a size D battery tossed out the window of a car going past me at 75 mph on the interstate. I've never had to walk a thirty-five-mile stretch wearing shoes two sizes too small. I've never been denied fifteen dollars because I couldn't attend seven days of revival meetings. I've never walked around a gas station showing pictures of my estranged daughter hoping, after all these years, someone might remember her. John recounted how Christians were normally harsh and judgmental, and just when I almost couldn't take any more, he told of a truck driver pulling over on a rainy night in Iowa and carrying him a long piece because another trucker had once done the same for him.

Turns out John came to Paradise looking for a place to shower and clean up, hoping to improve his odds of hitching a ride at the truck stop on the other side of town. I don't know if it was John's story or something else, but Rick went and made arrangements at the Motel 6 across the street. John and I continued talking outside the coffee shop, mostly him babbling in amazement and gratitude over someone doing such a thing and insisting on getting Rick's address so he could repay the favor. He could hardly remember the last time he had a genuine hot shower and a real bed to sleep in.

Rick's travels the next day would take him past the truck stop John wanted to get to, so he offered to pick John up at

Paradise early in the morning. I had my doubts if John would make it; just how reliable is a homeless guy traveling on foot to Oklahoma? Standing outside Paradise before Rick even arrived, John had his bag packed and was ready to roll. On the way to the truck stop, Rick informed John he had researched the bus schedule and found one leaving in a few hours from the terminal downtown direct to Oklahoma. He told John he was happy to take him to the truck stop and buy him the ticket but didn't want to presume he was up for a long bus trip. His choice: truck stop or bus station. John initially turned down the free ticket with the words "You've already done enough." Rick encouraged him to at least consider it; they were creeping along in morning traffic and had a few exits to go before passing the bus terminal. After a long silence, John spoke. He would take the bus to Oklahoma.

Hebrews 13:2 advises, "Do not forget to entertain strangers, for by so doing some people have entertained angels without knowing it" (NIV). Sometimes I wonder if John was an angel in a beaten-up baseball cap sent to a coffee shop in Tennessee because God knows my own salvation will never be complete until I am free to love when no one is looking or offering anything in return. God didn't want me to start a program for homeless people, launch a volunteer recruitment campaign at church, or raise money for the local mission—all things I am inclined to do. I think God just wanted me to see what would happen if one cold night I found myself face-to-face with a desperate stranger in need.

One of my favorite things to do is sit on a bench at the mall and watch people. Back when I traveled a lot, I got my fix in airports. It's amazing, maybe even disturbing, how you come to certain conclusions about people and their lives by studying their appearance or closely observing them for a few minutes out of the corner of your eye or over the top of your newspaper. It's not always easy, because things can get strange if people suspect you are watching them.

I've gotten pretty comfortable judging people by their outward appearances and actions, and when John stepped through the doors of Paradise, I sort of clicked and dragged him into my "homeless" file where people have earned their own misery. In that file you absolve yourself by simply telling such people you never give cash but you direct them to the local mission in your area. This most certainly would have been the option I would have chosen if it hadn't been for whatever was motivating the cigar-smoking tire salesman Rick to love people and God even when there's no one around to notice. Rick's operating system didn't have a homeless file. Apparently God's classification system is simpler than the complicated mess we employ; God accepts and loves all people because of who he is, not because of what they look like, have done, or haven't done.

I later asked Rick if he thought the guy was legit. His response was that the guy's legitimacy wasn't relevant to Rick's following the Spirit's leading. That got me to thinking, maybe as our relationship with Jesus grows, the mind of Christ becomes our own and walking in the kingdom of God becomes second nature, and our tendency toward judgment gives way to seeing people through Jesus's eyes.

Jesus seemed to personally love and serve those everyone else preferred to ignore or at least not hang around with. I'd rather pay some agency to do the dirty work for me while I remain at a safe and comfortable distance feeling good about myself. But Jesus did the dirty work himself. Okay, I know some hopeless people are unstable and belligerent, but so are some Baptist preachers I know. Most don't set out to be homeless. I have never known a single eight-year-old who answered the question "What do you want to be when you grow up?" with "Be a homeless person." For many it's just a series of difficult life situations, circumstances, bad decisions, and hardships until one cold February night they find themselves inside a little coffee shop in Tennessee looking for a ride to Oklahoma. Like John in Paradise.

I asked Rick for feedback on this chapter, and he expressed considerable reservation, saying that the chapter would perpetuate the "phantom Christian" phenomenon—the idea of someone who does the right thing every moment of every day. This phantom Christian phenomenon is usually described with some anecdotal story. In this case, it is the guy who befriends all homeless people, putting them up for the night, and passing out free bus tickets to every drifter passing through. Rick hopes you realize just how average a guy he is and that the real story is how incredibly compelling the love of God is in motivating him out of indifference and into action. Like Jesus said, "Why do you call me good? . . . No one is good—except God alone" (Mark 10:18 NIV). Millions of good deeds happen every day, so what makes Rick's different? Rick believes it's the motivation, and for Rick the motivation is Jesus's unconditional acceptance of and love for him. He's in good company with the apostle Paul, who said, "Christ's love compels us."

Rick also thought the chapter makes too much of John's being homeless, as if it's meant to stir up social activism or attention to the plight of the homeless. The truth is, I could have told stories of Rick's simply loving people God placed in closest proximity to him, such as his neighbors, coworkers, and customers.

The word *Christian* actually means "little Christ." Rick (and many other followers of Jesus) believes the risen living

Christ actually lives through him in the same way a vine's sap of life flows through a branch. We may be moral and right-eous, have fine ideals and beautiful thoughts, but without this presence of Christ overflowing, we Christians have lost our wind, fire, salt, and yeast. Perhaps loving the guy across the street is more where the rubber meets the road, given our natural tendency to go big or be an activist so we feel good. Certainly, *Guideposts* does not publish stories about some-body who simply loves those he comes across in the ebb and flow of everyday life. I've learned a lot about love from Rick because I've seen Christ loving others through him, even if it had no real value to onlookers.

For years, I ran with the elk (sometimes led the pack) who were convinced God wanted us to birth movements, shift paradigms, and save the world. Given the magnitude of it all, I didn't have the time, energy, or inclination to help the guy wandering into a coffee shop at closing time looking for a hot shower and a warm bed. I wonder if the good Samaritan story was a secret message to all tire salesmen, truckers, coffee-shop owners, cashiers, waitresses, carpet installers, UPS driv-ers, accountants, tech-heads, stay-at-home moms, working single moms, bartenders, barbers, and butchers to keep their eyes wide open, because the professionals are too pre-occupied with grander things, passing by real people with needs God placed right beneath their noses in everyday life. Maybe J. R. R. Tolkien was onto something when he wrote in *The Lord of the Rings*, "The road must be trod, but it will be very hard. And neither strength nor wisdom will carry us far upon it. This quest may be attempted by the weak with as much hope as the strong. Yet such is oft the course of deeds that move the wheels of the world; small hands do them, while the eyes of the great are elsewhere."

Though unknown to me at the time, I partly relied on Christianity to make a name for myself through helping and serving people (or at least running organizations and ministries that had people who did). Loving the folks in my cul-de-sac wasn't good enough. I had to do something bigger and more spectacular. I mean, come on, how many people do you know who went off on a spiritual retreat and returned with the grand vision of getting to know the people in their neighborhood?

Some will take offense at all this, saying it conveniently excuses people from caring about the plight of people on the other side of one's city or world. I'm starting to think God has this figured out better than we realize. What if Rick types are spread out over the entire planet? And what if these Ricks weren't too preoccupied with themselves, their ministry, their church, or their organization to see people God placed along their path? What if these Ricks took Jesus's message of love seriously even when there was no one else around to applaud it? And what if these Ricks, when faced with needs beyond their ability, called on other Ricks to pitch in for a while? I've experienced my share of ministry-model and cutting-edge strategies, but I'm not sure anything works any better than that. If life caves in on me and things happen to me that I never imagined in my wildest dreams, and if one cold night I'm desperate enough to walk inside a coffee shop not knowing where else to turn for help, I hope one of those Ricks will be there.

(E)pilogue

I'm MORE AWARE OF GOD THESE DAYS. IT ONCE SEEMED I had to go searching for God and needed religion to find him. Turns out he was searching for me. No more striving to find him, just believing he found me. In my disillusionment with institutional church, I contemplated chucking Christianity, but I discovered that these were two separate and not nearly equal things. Seeing I needed a little help to get this, God sent a variety pack of characters who communicated his truth to me in the ways he knew I needed to hear it. Sometimes it took people smeared in axle grease or sporting body piercings and tattoos to unplug my ears and open my eyes. Conditioned to expect God in church buildings and worship services, I never figured on running into him at the Waffle House.

I've learned you can be technically right about God in seminary classes and church pews but still not really know him. I'm noticing my brainy theological explanations about God are giving way to very personal ones. God is opening my eyes to see I could be someone else's divine nobody by depending on him to prompt me when someone stumbles into the coffee shop at closing time or allowing him to transform my eyes into his, helping me see people as he does, instead of judging them by their music or who they voted for. Others might not see value in it, but God is and has always been secretly building his kingdom one person at a time through the likes of tire salesmen, drummers, and mechanics.

After giving up on ever doing anything spectacular for God, I found the time and freedom to develop close relationships with a few believers who have become dear to me. Some of us gather together regularly and celebrate the Lord's Supper. Adults and children huddle together in a front room, and the gospel comes alive once again through sharing bread and wine, reminding us of Christ's life within, his unconditional acceptance and sufficiency, and our need to depend on him.

Some days "mission" means making myself available to my neighbors out in the front yard raking leaves. I have found there's more hurt and need in my cul-de-sac than I ever imagined. Occasionally I'll come in contact with someone who remembers me as the seminary graduate making a name for myself in ministry. Without fail they ask, "Are you still a pastor?" I never know quite how to answer. I once was the senior pastor of a growing evangelical church. Years later I set out to start a progressive, postmodern, relational kind of church. What I eventually discovered is that changing worship styles, outreach strategies, and sermon topics was sort of like deciding whether you would like your egg poached, scrambled, over-easy, sunny-side up, or raw—it's still an egg.

If being a "pastor" means deeply desiring that others know God, walk in the freedom of his grace, be transformed through their relationship with his indwelling life, all the while experiencing his kingdom in the present, I guess I'm oriented that way. I have misgivings using the term in reference to myself. For many it carries too much misconstrued baggage. I'm just

Jim—flawed, imperfect, maybe a little crazy, just a guy who wants to know Jesus better himself.

Pressing forward, sometimes falteringly, there are days when discouragement sets in and I feel I'm wandering around in circles. I think I understand Peter's description of being "aliens and strangers in the world" and often feel this way even among church people. Whatever the future holds, I have my own intimately personal mustard seed of faith that God is real, present, and much more interested in me than I am in him.

He whispers to me in the wind, "I AM what you're looking for."

(e)pilogue

SOME MEMORIES YOU CARRY AROUND INSIDE YOU LIKE pieces of broken glass. I remember sitting spellbound as a little boy watching my mother in the kitchen work her magic arranging flowers. Hidden beneath sweaters and blankets in her dresser drawers were sketches, paintings, and poems I sometimes dug out to look at when she wasn't home. It's a shame my mother rarely used and enjoyed her artistic gift. This is but one of countless cruelties I wish away about her sad life. Who knows what other wonderful qualities she had before the sorrow and bottle stole them away. Somehow her creativity was born in me. I sometimes think of her when I'm on autumn walks collecting leaves to arrange across the fireplace mantel, or picking spring flowers to exhibit in a vase. I learned from my mother that a person never has to go far to find something beautiful if he or she has eyes to see.

Failing to rescue my mother from her depression was unquestionably the greatest heartache of my childhood. Her happiness was my foremost longing and heaviest burden; some days I still carry it, but more and more I'm learning to let Jesus carry it. I love Mom, but it's a love that hurts deeply.

I once asked her if she thought she'd go to heaven when she died. She replied, "I hope so." I hope so too. I'm sure the theology of this is not quite right, but maybe somehow on the other side she and I will get a do-over.

Acknowledgments

GOD USED THE WRITING OF THIS BOOK TO DEEPEN MY LIFE in him, and I am grateful for all those who were part of the process. There are a few who were particularly instrumental in helping make it all happen.

Greg Daniel of W Publishing Group read between the lines of some ramblings I sent him one day via e-mail, which eventually took shape in the *Divine Nobodies* title, theme, and book. I learned that the difference between an average writer and a good one is all the editing and rewrite suggestions that Greg and others at W provided. Now, if I can only become a *great* writer. Well, they can only do so much.

Rick Harris was invaluable in offering detailed feedback along the way, and you would thank him if you read some of the first drafts of chapters that had a way of meandering into the muck and mire of my brilliant but utterly incoherent ruminations. Special thanks also go to all those divine nobodies who generously gave input.

My most cherished divine nobody appears sparingly in the book—my wife, Pam. There are so many different ways God uses her to press me deeper into the truth about myself and my relationship with God. Pam's unwillingness to compromise truth significantly influenced the contents of this book. Those times I was prone to exaggerate or spout off some view that sounded nice but didn't really fit where I was, she caught as only a truth-loving spouse of eight years can.

About the Author

Jim Palmer offers guidance as a pastor, speaker, writer, blogger, and conversationalist to people seeking to know God in deeper and more expansive ways. He is the founder of the Pilgrimage Project, an initiative encouraging the freedom to imagine, dialogue, live, and express new possibilities for being an authentic Christian. Jim lives in Nashville with his wife, Pam, and daughter, Jessica, and can be contacted at www.divinenobodies.com.